Totally Jed!
the Third

Ted Sherrell was born and educated in West Devon, he has had an interesting and most diverse working career; past work including being a civil servant, newspaper reporter, fireman, factory worker, door-to-door salesman, insurance agent, shopkeeper, proofreader and as a business adviser  calling principally on farms in Devon and Cornwall.

A farmer's son, he has worked amongst and been around the farming and rural communities of Devonshire for most of his life. He draws greatly upon this background – plus his various working experiences – when writing his novels and short stories.

In past years he gained an Honours Degree in History through a correspondence course and, as well as his writing career, Ted Sherrell was for many years involved in local government as a member of Tavistock Town Council, where in 2013 he was made the first ever Freeman of Tavistock. He has also been a member of West Devon Borough Council and is a Justice of the Peace.

With My Warmest Best Wishes

Ted Sherrell

Also by Ted Sherrell:

Totally Ted!
The Third

A Third Dose of Witty Reflections on Modern Life from
a Grumpy Old Westcountry Man

Ted Sherrell

Illustrations by
BECKY SHEPPARD

UNITED WRITERS
Cornwall

UNITED WRITERS PUBLICATIONS LTD
Ailsa, Castle Gate, Penzance, Cornwall.
www.unitedwriters.co.uk

British Library Cataloguing in Publication Data:
A catalogue record for this book is
available from the British Library.

ISBN 9781852002077

Printed and bound in Great Britain by
United Writers Publications Ltd.,
Cornwall.

To my beloved Ann, my wonderful
wife and so cherished friend
and to
my treasured family, all of whom make
my life so rich and fulfilling.

The *Totally Ted!* columns appear weekly in
Tavistock, Okehampton, East & Mid-Devon and
East Cornwall newspapers.

Contents

1

Downsizing

𝓐 FEW weeks back, Ann and I were sitting relaxing in our front room, she a glass of Australian wine in her hand, myself a generous dollop of the Scottish 'Amber Nectar'. Suddenly she looked at me, then said gently but with an air of decisiveness, a word which transformed the whisky in my mouth to hemlock and sent an arctic chill down my rather (these days) curved spine: 'We really need to consider downsizing,' said she, 'and in the relatively near future.'

A couple of years before she had mentioned such during the flow of a casual somewhat desultory conversation, but back then it was clearly a prophecy of ultimate inevitability not a statement of policy.

The problem with her words now were simply that in terms of imminence she was right; in so many aspects of life, working, personal and domestic decisions have to be made, 'nettles' need to be grasped and action taken. Prevarication, something at which I am a master, must be slain.

We have lived in our much loved house for over 45

years; mind you it was in a lamentable state when we bought it.

The plus side here is that had the property been in half decent fettle then there is no way we would have been able to afford it.

Over the decades, slowly but assuredly and persistently, we have carried out multiple improvements or, to be exact, Ann with the help occasionally of a builder has done so. I would not wish to dwell in any home where a total incompetent such as myself has played any part in its potential upgrading.

Now, largely thanks to her vision, hard work and tenacity it is an abode of comfort, style and individuality and has fine uninterrupted views down over the Crowndale Valley (including the birthplace of Sir Francis Drake).

We both enjoy our house (where we raised our four sons) immensely and in an ideal world would happily see out our days here. Also it has the practical present day plusses of standing opposite a well known local nursing home, whilst about half a mile from the back of our abode lies the town cemetery. Possibly a morbid way of viewing matters but at our age such realism cannot be ignored.

There are problems however; the garden is large. When bringing up the family this was an asset as there was sufficient leeway for the kicking of a football. For several years after, too, we appreciated the generous space around the house, but now, with increasing age, we find the challenge of keeping it under control ever more onerous, stressful, and truthfully this also applies to the dwelling itself.

Having brought it up to a sound standard of comfort and repair, we find it ever more exacting and expensive keeping it there.

Furthermore, our council tax and utility bills have swollen appreciably in recent times, whereas being now largely retired our incomes have not, thus inevitably we are going to have to make major and painful decisions.

Quite soon, assuredly, we'd find the theory of moving house is very different from the fraught, taxing even traumatic realities of actually doing it, made even more mind concentrating when one is downsizing.

Our next home, whether it be cottage, bungalow, chalet, mobile home or even camper van will be appreciably smaller than our present one (though in theory our savings should receive a healthy boost).

There will be hard decisions to make as to what furniture to retain and how to dispose of that jettisoned; then there are the drawers, a seeming multitude of them, mostly packed.

I'm largely to blame for this, for whilst Ann is quite pragmatic when it comes to retaining items, I'm very much of the 'it might come in useful sometime' school of thought. If one practises this for almost half a century then such junk accrues.

Books too; we both being avid readers, Ann especially, we have almost enough to stock a shop. And this is only the start of it.

Estate agents have to be involved, plus surveyors to affirm we are not riddled with radon gas and the house is not constructed over a mine shaft. Not least, of course, is the locating and purchasing at the right price of our new domicile.

'*I think there may be a problem selling your house, sir.*'

The entire project is somewhat terrifying when contemplated now.

Undoubtedly Ann is correct in suggesting we give serious thought regarding seeking a smaller residence, but clearly we must not rush into it. My indolent nature suggests to me that probable action on this front should take place 'dreckly' – to an idle man this particular Devonshire word is priceless.

2

The Public Conveniences

*I*T is said that there are two certainties in this life – death and taxes. Mind you, observation would suggest that this is not entirely accurate; whilst none of us (as far as I am aware) has yet mastered the art of avoiding the 'grim reaper', there are those, often of very ample means, most adept at sidestepping that which is due to Her Majesty's Revenue and Customs.

In everyday living, however, there are universal matters which come the way of we human beings which are essential to the continuation of our much valued lives; most prominent amongst them, obviously, are eating and drinking.

The former is that which acts as fuel to our active bodies, the latter staves off dehydration. With this in mind, there is another function within our anatomy which must be honoured daily – the jettisoning of the solids and liquids surplus to that which our stomachs need, or with which they can cope. In other words, visits to the lavatory need to be made on a very regular basis, irrespective of our being a rich man, poor man, beggar man or thief; in this there is full social and gender equality.

Being a fellow who has never stinted on his food and has always imbibed liberally – tea, coffee and alcohol alike (though rarely water, except with Alka-Seltzer when trying to rectify overindulgence) – I have always been a most loyal frequenter of the 'smallest room' in the house.

Now, as age advances, my bladder appears to delight in contracting further with every added year and my doddering forays to the loo, both day and night, are negotiated at ever decreasing intervals.

Whilst such a routine is relatively easy to maintain when one is at home, when out and about there can be major problems. Not so much when travelling, to be fair; for if on an aircraft, coach or train, adequate facilities are usually provided whilst, if in a car, motorway service stations, on the whole, provide toilets and personal cleansing areas of exemplary cleanliness, maintenance, general ambience and privacy.

The situation in numerous towns and cities, however, is all too often very different. Being well aware that whilst they should provide public conveniences for residents and visitors alike, but are not, by law, compelled to do so, many local authorities have been easing their own strained finances by closing down many – at times all – of these vital centres of personal relief. Thus it is not unusual these days when in a location with which one is unfamiliar, to cede to the demands of one's bladder and hastily seek out the 'holy grail' of amenity signs, only to have hopes dashed, when on arriving at the relevant potential sanctuary, one finds them locked up.

Rapidly adopting the philosophy of 'when needs must, the devil drives', one searches urgently for the nearest pub or café (preferably the former), then, somewhat embarrassed, comb the premises for their facilities. The problem with this is that, having taken advantage of their hospitality, most of us would feel an obligation to purchase a drink – tea, coffee, or alcohol – before leaving. Thus, a couple of hours hence – possibly less – confrontation with porcelain becomes a priority once more.

Mind you, if locating a community privy – and one of acceptable sanitation is becoming an escalating challenge in this country, beyond our shores it can be worse, often infinitely so. Even in the generally sophisticated lands of Western Europe, the overall standard of such essential amenities is often inferior to ours in terms of both hygiene and availability. The further east or south one travels, the worse can be the experience. There are numerous countries and areas of the world where I have never set foot, and am unlikely to do so now; however, during occasional visits to states beyond Europe there was a lesson which I soon learned – never leave one's hotel having eaten or imbibed more than the bare necessity until one returned.

If such cities had public conveniences at all (and many appeared not to) they were so often a lifeline only for the desperate. The worst places ever I recall were Lhasa, Tibet and Kathmandu in Nepal.

Only extreme distress would entice anybody into their urinals; as to the communal WCs, had I needed to use one I would have dived into a temple – of which there were many – and prayed fervently for the deliverance that would be instant constipation.

3

Father's Day

THERE is little doubt that at times a measure of anti-Americanism exists in our country – across the wider world also, for that matter. When saying this I refer, of course, to the United States, not to the entire continent.

To some extent there has always been some discord between our 'two nations divided by a common language' as was said perceptively by, I believe, George Bernard Shaw; divided, also to a degree, by history – after all, they did fight a war against us for their independence.

In terms of geography and meteorology, as well, there is a vast difference – theirs is a colossal land – with climates varying from the tropical to, almost, the Arctic. Ann and I have made several visits during the past 20 years, our son Matthew, daughter-in-law, Avisa, and their three children having lived (and still residing) in New York for work purposes during this time. We enjoy our stays with them – their company and their hospitality have made many a treasured memory, although sadly, but inevitably, there has been no opportunity for us all to get together during the covid crisis.

To us, however, there is something in the American way of life and overall character which does not quite gel; perhaps, to a degree, it is their insularity; with the exception of North Korea (where the unfortunate citizens are given no option) it is doubtful if there is another race on earth with less interest in, and knowledge of, the outside world, than that which dwells in the 50 states which constitute 'the land of the free'. Yet, despite their apparent lack of interest in the peoples, cultures and ways of life of the 200 plus countries which are to be found around the globe, the inhabitants of a multitude of these sovereign states have, conversely, long been fascinated by many facets of American customs and values.

Assuredly we are not immune from such influence in our islands. So many 'Americanisms' have crept into our precious language – the horrible 'hi' and 'ok' being well to the fore; this is probably inevitable as English, worldwide, is the principle – and largely universal – language 'spoken' by computers; sadly, however, it is the transatlantic version of our noble tongue which holds sway in this field. The insightful words of playwright Shaw have come home to roost.

Then there is the culture, the grip on our eating and leisure habits which have crossed the ocean: McDonald's and KFC, Hollywood films, jazz and rap music, and so much more shapes the way we live. Fair enough, we are free to embrace which we like and ignore that which we do not. There are customs, too, some of which I detest. Hallowe'en, imported from the States, is my supreme 'Bête Noire'; to me it is an abomination; the glorification of witches and devils, and the manifest celebration of much that is evil. It goes further; a vast crop of pumpkins and suchlike, not grown for the benefit of people in a world where so many go hungry, but rather to be purged into the making of hideous lanterns; the entire cynical charade would surely not be missed, except by greengrocers, supermarkets and others seeking to make a 'fast buck'.

It is, though, time for a touch of positivity. For we in Britain have taken to our hearts a tradition which is celebrated on the third Sunday in June – Father's Day. Mother's Day – or Mothering Sunday as is the correct title – is an ancient British custom (whether solely, or not, I am unsure) going back centuries. The honouring of the male parent, however, began in the United States and to me is a most welcome addition to the relatively limited number of annual days which we celebrate formally and when gifts are bestowed.

Amongst my good fortunes in life is that my dear wife Ann has blessed us with four fine sons. Miserable, moaning toad that I am, they never forget me on the day devoted to Fathers – even grumpy ones.

All send cards, each of which represent their individual personalities; this is so on every occasion. There will be a sentimental offering, one of humour, a quite formal greeting and an artistic contribution. Even if they did not sign them, I would be aware of whom had forwarded which.

What they also send, or drop off, are life giving elixirs with the medical name 'single malt', plus health enhancing solids made by those pharmaceutical giants, Thorntons and Cadbury.

When in office President Trump enacted sanctions against many nations, denying them exports from his country. It is a relief he never made any attempt to interfere with the custom of goodwill and bounty which comes the way of we Dads every June. Long may it continue.

4

Humour & Wit

*D*URING this difficult era in which we live – though, if truth be told, throughout all history folk have dwelt in testing times – humour and wit are priceless, crucial ingredients to be thrown into the mixing bowl of experience, habits, beliefs, actions, work and social interaction which influences, perhaps even shapes human behaviour.

Mind you, when I write of such levity, in my view I articulate a brace of diverse aspects of amusing communication – although, on occasions, only subtle nuance divides them.

Humour, to a large extent, could be said to be a professional matter; comedians, comic actors, actresses and the like are the mainspring of such, usually via the media, comprehensive in this age – though by way of cinema and theatre also. They are there to entertain us, to elevate our spirits. In accord with personal taste, some succeed, whilst others merely bore.

Some in this field have the crucial gift of spontaneity, but one feels they are in the minority. For few will venture onto our television screens, or on stage, without a catalogue of rehearsed jokes and asides planted in their minds, much of the materials supplied to them by script writers and the like.

There are those, of course, who could ad-lib a performance but one feels there is far from an abundance of such. With TV 'sit coms', their success (or failure) can be down to the writer's craft, plus the ability of actors to convert the amusing situations – even absurdities – that permeate everyday life into an art form which entertains and raises the spirits.

Wit though, as I see it, is different – more personal, and unrehearsed. The ability to bring forth virtually instantly, a retort, usually amusing, to a comment made to them, or an observation of an aspect – at times bizarre – of human behaviour. Such sharp quips – sometimes of an acerbic nature – are as likely to come from quick witted men and women 'in the street' as they are from those who entertain for a living.

Relatively few, however, are recorded for posterity. Thus 'off the cuff' witty comments and barbs – which they are – almost inevitably will have been uttered by folk of some eminence, plus, on occasions, naturally, those professionals in the field of entertainment.

Within the former group, Sir Winston Churchill looms large. He mouthed some, of a searing nature, which remain oft quoted. Among the best was one to a lady MP in the Commons with whom he shared a mutual dislike. This woman, in the midst of a bitter exchange with the great man, said, 'Sir, if you were my husband I would put poison in your tea,'; The sublime rejoinder? 'Madam, if you were my wife I would drink it.' Another barbed retaliatory thrust from him, was to a lady, a member of the opposition, when clearly he had imbibed somewhat liberally; confronting him, she said, 'Sir, you're drunk,' to which instantly the robust reply – 'Madam, you're ugly, but I shall be sober in the morning.' Also in the world of politics, there was a masterful, though rancorous, retort from that eminent statesman, Ernest Bevin: to a friend who commented that Herbert Morrison, with whom Bevin was always at odds in the cabinet, 'was his own worst enemy' came the immediate repost, 'Not whilst I'm alive he's not.'

The literary world, as might be expected, possessed (and still does) a plethora of writers whose minds were razor sharp. The brilliant Oscar Wilde when, at a port, was asked if there was anything he wished to declare, quipped 'Only my genius'.

That famed American author, Mark Twain, when told a newspaper had published his obituary in the mistaken belief he had passed away, commented, laconically, 'Reports of my death have been greatly exaggerated.'

One of my favourite cynically droll remarks was uttered by Hollywood star, the late Mickey Rooney. Once, in interview, his interrogator mentioned that he, Rooney, had married nine times. When asked to comment, the actor gave no reasons for him being a serial groom and divorcee, but pointed out, simply, he had weddings down to a fine art. Said he, 'I always marry early of a morning, so if it doesn't work out, I've not wasted the entire day.'

Still, although a mite unkind, as good a spontaneous witticism I've heard recently was out in the street. It was uttered by a young fellow to his mate as, on a narrowish pavement, they came up behind a couple of gigantic girth, strolling side by side. Assessing the prodigious barrier to their progress, he reflected, 'We will need a packed lunch if we've got to walk all around this pair.'

5

Taxing Times

ONE day back in March, one of the Royal Mail's ever helpful, courteous and hard-working postal workers thrust four communications through our letter box. The timing was perfect, as I had just made some coffee; thus Ann and I could digest the news, good or bad, which had come our way, along with biscuits and a good strong black brew.

We sat at the kitchen table and surveyed the mail; one item was a leaflet which was set aside to peruse later; there was also a clothes catalogue addressed to Ann; such arrived, from the same company, about once a fortnight – unsolicited. It was instantly set aside for recycling unopened. Not that the range of ladies clothes and fashions displayed within its glossy pages were unattractive, it was just that the average garment within was usually the price of a decent second-hand car.

There were two further envelopes, one white and addressed to us both, the other brown and marked for me. Fair division of labour decreed she opened that which was joint, which she did with alacrity; to say she screamed when

b

studying its contents would be something of an exaggeration but there was upon her face an expression of horror and when she spoke, her voice was the prisoner of shock and disbelief. 'It's the council tax,' she gasped. 'It is truly horrendous.'

I took the sheet from her and scanned the figures displayed. Instantly I realised that the steaming bean-laden beverage which awaited us was totally inadequate – brandy was required and a goodly amount of it. For emblazoned upon the demand was a sum akin to that which one imagines would be paid on Windsor Castle, perhaps with Buckingham Palace thrown in as well, and as we remain several bands below this area's top and most expensive level it struck me as unlikely that I was the only citizen of Tavistock and its surrounds currently contemplating a mid-morning pick-me-up.

My many years as a councillor gave me insight as to why – to a degree at least – we here in Devon pay one of the highest levies in the land. It is known as the 'sparsity factor'; it is a large county, predominantly rural and lightly populated, but possesses the highest mileage of roads of any authority in the country; all of which have to be maintained at public expense. Also, more recycling bins can be emptied in a city in half an hour than can be accessed in half a day on the likes of Dartmoor. Attempts to rationalise this latest bill, however, could in no way mitigate the fact that for the next year a very solid chunk of our income was now accounted for.

So not the best start to the day. Wearily I picked up the brown envelope and opened it. This contained better news, for it gave details of my state pension entitlement for the financial year about to begin. There was to be a modest

*Perhaps my meagre pensison increase of 25p
will pay for a trip to the beauty salon.*

increase – a touch over the level of inflation – which was to be welcomed. My eyes wandered downwards over the detailed information sheet – a somewhat desultory scan until they alighted upon the sentence printed at the bottom. Metaphorically speaking, they 'lit up'; for there lay glad tidings of great joy – the promise of wealth to come.

In December of this year, if I still have a pulse, this grumpy old toad will have blighted this world for eight decades; miserable old so-and-so though I am, I will still receive extra reward from the state for the good fortune of attaining such longevity.

There in bold print it informed me I was to receive an increase in my pension – one which could be used as a major ally when confronting the council tax assault; weekly, my pension would increase by – 25 pence. Thus in just three weeks I would gain sufficient extra revenue to be able to afford the first class stamp necessary to fund the sending of a letter to the council complaining about their chilling charge; such joy!

In somewhat jaundiced mood, I looked at the leaflet which I had 'saved' for later. This concentrated the mind; for it was an ad extolling the virtues of a care home. It was not addressed specifically to either of us, but I have not the slightest doubt that being the doddery, pedantic, ever more confused old fool that I am, I would be a vastly more suitable candidate than Ann.

I have to say there was little in the blurb that appealed – certainly not the promise of a hair and beauty salon, social activities and access to WiFi (whatever that is). I've seen Ann reading it as well; hopefully this was purely out of curiosity, but, of course, it could have been intended to keep me on my toes. I do hope neither of us will need to avail ourselves of their services for many a long day – if ever.

6

The Page I Turn to First

*A*MONGST the foremost highlights of my week is the obtaining, on a Thursday morning, of the *Tavistock Times Gazette*. Once a copy is in my hands I know that the world as we know it still spins without deviation on its axis, and despite Covid-19, climate change, political turbulence throughout the world, plus the constant stresses imposed on we fans by a particularly infuriating sports club known as Plymouth Argyle FC, life remains well worth living.

With this in mind, I commence my perusal of this excellent local paper on page 2 – the front cover lead story saved for later; for it could be argued that the information displayed on the second page is possibly the most important and relevant in the paper. This is the sheet which lists many of the week's hatched, matched and dispatched.

The first two categories are of significance, of course, and, to me, of some interest. It is, after all, good, happy tidings reading of those who have just entered the world; likewise to observe reports of unions involving love. However, this brace of groupings which exude positivity is almost invariably outnumbered – often greatly so – by the list that is the 'dispatched'.

To say I scan such with interest would be a major understatement; for I have reached an age when disclosure as to those who have 'shuffled off' can concentrate the mind. Starting every day checking I still have a pulse, I nonetheless run my eyes down the columns and get quite nervous when the letter 'S' is reached. A sense of relief courses through me when there is no mention of either myself or any of our clan. Certainly I've no desire at present to be sent up to be interviewed by St Peter or, possibly more likely, to be dispatched down to the fiery kingdom of 'Old Nick' himself. I'd not greatly welcome the latter, but as a man who has the 'blood of a lizard' and can shiver in a heatwave, it could have compensations.

After this initial somewhat cursory study of the names of the folk just departed, over a cup of coffee I will give it my full attention. Firstly, is there anybody I know mentioned of whose passing I was unaware? More often than not, the answer is yes; having lived in the area all of my days, it is almost inevitable that folk I know – or have known – will have passed on. Some will be of similar age to myself. 'They're taking them out of our pen now,' as my farmer father would comment ruefully when any friend of his of like vintage passed away.

Certainly I find that my purchase of condolence cards increases by the year. All are sent to their relatives with a genuine sense of deep sympathy; after all, virtually all in this world have family, perhaps also close friends, who love them. If, however, they have lived long, fulfilling lives, their leaving of this world, whilst sad and often upsetting, rarely will be tragic.

There are those, though, who are taken before their time; they may have been killed in an accident with no chance to say goodbye, or as a result of a lost battle against some callous illness. Distressingly it is not unusual to read of the heart-breaking demise of such young men and women who leave not just grieving parents and a spouse, but young children for whom the loss of a mum or dad will be devastating and inevitably, in diverse ways, life changing.

It is when I read such tragic notices that I realise that I, who have lived well beyond the span stated in the Bible of 'three score years and ten', have so much to be grateful for. Whilst my health is far from perfect, I still am able to live a tolerably active and most fulfilling life and have the priceless bonus of sharing it with my beloved wife Ann.

As to the future, mind you, who knows what it has in store. In this direction, William Shakespeare is not encouraging; for in his play, 'As you like it', he has the character, Jaques, articulating the seven ages of mankind from the initial lifting of the curtain that is life until it drops, finally. The first age is the infant, mewing and puking in his nurse's arms; the final one, which I am very close to – indeed, might well have reached – is described in disturbing fashion as, 'second childishness and mere oblivion; sans teeth, sans eyes, sans taste, sans everything.' Not an agreeable prospect; however, there is only one way to avoid it and that is an appointment with the undertaker. I'm not keen – at present.

7

The Bible or the Land

*T*HAT illustrious, highly regarded churchman, Archbishop Desmond Tutu was well to the fore in the fight in South Africa against apartheid some 40 years ago. He was articulate as well as forthright and courageous when it came to the oppression (and inequality) of black and Asian communities by the white, originally European, minority in the Republic.

Although a committed Christian and a very senior member of the church hierarchy he once cynically reflected on the teachings of Jesus that 'When the white missionaries came to Africa, they had the Bible and we had the land. They said, 'let us pray'; we closed our eyes. When again we opened them, we had the Bible and they had the land.

There is, in a sense, much truth in this acerbic but perceptive barbed comment and much of the responsibility for this, it could be argued, lies in the innocent, deeply felt teachings of Jesus. Not that Jesus wished to acquire acreage or wealth; the opposite, in fact. What he desired of people is that, essentially, they love one another, have zealous eyes for justice, fairness and respect – indeed, view everyone and everything with goodwill, whilst pursuing lives of peace.

The complication regarding the noble principles by which Christ lived and his constant uncompromising ministrations to all who followed him or heard his words, is that he was not the same as others; he was the son of God – thus, in reality, could never truly comprehend the frailties, foolishness and selfishness inherent in the bulk of humankind. In that sense, even though two millennia has passed since he walked the earth, little has ever changed regarding human nature and behaviour.

So often over the centuries men and women of deep and genuine belief in the teachings of the Bible have, over a period of time, moved away, without realising it, from the honourable worthy teachings of that good book. An example of this are the people similar to the missionaries spoken of by Archbishop Tutu – the first English folk to settle in North America: The Pilgrim Fathers who sailed from Plymouth in 1620.

Devout puritans, they sailed for the New World in order to be able to practise their Christian beliefs free from persecution by the state. One can imagine that they could have been easy prey for the Native Americans, seeing as they came more as refugees than as missionaries. The reality though was that they were largely left unharmed by the indigenous peoples, and in fact, the tribes, used to the way of life and the harsh climate and terrain, often helped their new neighbours to survive. For their part the pious incomers, obedient to the guidance of Jesus, tried, with some success, to spread his word and his teachings.

It was not that long, however, before the more worldly and avaricious, whilst still paying some lip service to the spreading of the Gospels, began to acquire the vast lands – for themselves – over which the native folk had roamed and hunted for generations. By the late nineteenth century Native Americans were largely restricted to reservations on poor land, in both the United States and Canada; they, like the tribes of Africa, had the Bible, but the rich land plus oil, minerals and such like, was mainly in the ownership of the incoming Europeans.

Yet despite being the serial sceptic that I am, I would have to concede that those who use the Bible as a useful tool are only part of the story; for there have been many – some famed – who truly have spread, and lived by the word of Jesus, and who have dedicated themselves to the well-being and care of the downtrodden, persecuted and neglected on this globe.

David Livingstone was a missionary who devoted his life to the service of the people of Africa and did much towards eradicating the evil slave trade. Albert Schweitzer, again in Africa, set up his famous hospital at Lambarene where, amongst other diseases, he waged war on leprosy and sleeping sickness.

Eric Liddell, the great Scottish Olympic sprinter of Chariots of Fire fame, turned his back on celebrity status and, with Bible in hand, went off to serve the people of China; he was subsequently killed by the Japanese. Then, of course, in slightly more recent times, there was Mother Theresa, a nun who committed her life to caring for the sick and desperately poor of Calcutta.

Many other good men and women, past and present,

motivated only by the Bible and teachings of Jesus, come to mind in terms of noble service to others.

So for once in my life, an attitude somewhat dominated by negativity, must be set aside positively to state that in this world there has always been, and remains, men and women who represent the finest of the teachings of Jesus Christ; to them, clearly, the Bible is more valuable than the land.

8

The Census

WE agreed, Ann and I, that as she does the vast bulk of
the housework, cooking, DIY, gardening, washing
and ironing, sending of birthday cards and general
correspondence to family and friends, shopping, sewing
plus perceptive, thoughtful planning regarding our
negotiation of life's boulder strewn path, I, when the time
came, would fill out the census form.

Seeing as it plops on the front door mat but once every
ten years, I can say no other than I do feel I get by far the
better of the deal. Thus when the envelope marked
'Census 2021' came through the letter box, I, like a coiled
spring, grabbed it, ready for instant action. It was,
however, not to be.

Picking it up, I thought it to be somewhat smaller than
I had expected; for this there was a reason – it was not a
form as such, to be filled out, but rather an invitation
(though command would be a more apt word to use as by
law a representative of every household in the land has to
complete one) to go online to answer the manifold and
myriad questions regarding the lives, customs, habits,

ethnicity, ages and so much more of all residing in that dwelling on March 21st.

Now the chances of this Luddite dinosaur going online are even less than Argyle's prospects regarding making the Champions League in the near future. I scanned the instructions for several minutes and, at last, in small print (clearly not really meant to be seen) it gave a number to phone if one wanted a paper form to fill in. With some alacrity I dialled the number; the exercise was both easy and efficient – a voice told me I would be sent a 'proper form' (my description as I trust only pen and paper when it comes to documentation) within five working days; and to give credit where it is due, it was.

Mind you, to call it a form was an understatement; it was a tome the size of a present day phone book. My heart sank; this was a task and challenge which could take days to overcome; perhaps I might not conquer it at all. Mustering all the willpower I possess – not a lot – and invoking the 'Dunkirk Spirit', I ripped open the envelope and surveyed its contents.

There were instructions, then a 32 page log to fill in. However, considerable relief engulfed me when I realised I would only have to attack forty per cent of it; for the document allowed for there to be up to five inhabitants in the dwelling. As there are only the two of us, thus just a brace needed to be addressed.

Most assuredly, it was minutely detailed. There was more interrogation regarding one's dwelling than would come from the average estate agent were we trying to sell it. As a gent I know opined to me, 'They want to know the ins and outs of a cat's behind' – although he did not use the term 'behind'. Names, ages, religion, occupation, gender.

On to the section devoted to ethnic groups; here 1 was disappointed, for whilst a multitude were listed nowhere was I able to tick 'Devonian' or, for Ann, who was born in Padstow, 'Cornish'. A query I did not answer accurately was the one regarding my mastery of English; I stated that I spoke it 'very well'. The reality though is that I mumble in a Devonshire accent and use a vast array of dialect words which few beyond our region would understand.

There were sections which bemused, none more than – and I quote – 'Question 17: Deliberately left blank; Go to 18'. Ours not to reason why. For our 10 month old great-grandson, Edward, there was good news; again I quote 'Those under 1 year old do not need to answer Question 13'. He would have found it hard to get his little fingers around a pen and I'm not sure if completing the form in crayon would be allowable. Having said this, with children so savvy when it comes to technology, it could be that even now he could do something beyond the capabilities of his great-grandfather – going online.

The filling out of this massive, comprehensive missive was not that onerous although it did tend to be tedious. Clearly, though, it has to be done for governments, councils and institutions generally have to know the size, complexity and diversity of the people who inhabit these islands. Hopefully Ann and I will still be about when the next one comes along; one thing is for certain though – if I am still here I will not have mastered 'online'.

9

What is this Life?

'WHAT is this life if full of care, we have no time to stand and stare.' So wrote poet William Henry Davies well over a century ago lamenting the rush and bustle that was life then and which, increasingly, has dominated our world and existence ever since – until March 2020, that is. For then, literally overnight, we were 'locked down' to varying degrees due to the vile Coronavirus. Granted life is slowly returning to something approaching normality but we have not reached it yet – if we ever do.

For sure, however, these past 15 months of restrictions have left so very many of us with time on our hands – probably more than we have ever known in our lives, no matter how long these have lasted. So what during these torrid, often alarming times have we been doing? Have we taken the poet's advice and stood and stared? Statistics suggest that we most certainly have – but not quite in the way which he envisaged.

For his take on things, his ideas as to how we inhabitants of our magnificent islands should pause our hectic, involved, often stressful lives, were based on folk gazing about themselves at the beauties and, often, wonders of the natural world around them; to him people could find peace and fulfilment – certainly eschew stress – by absorbing the tranquillity and nobility of so much which surrounds us.

The problem is that whilst his insightful words have in a sense resonated with great numbers of the British citizenry, it has not quite been in the fashion and field he was advocating. Great numbers have indeed stared – but rarely in a standing position and even more infrequently in the open air, taking in the visual delights of the world about us which can refresh body, mind and soul.

For statistics put out recently suggest that a wide swathe of the population of the United Kingdom – of all ages – have spent, during the period of Covid-19, on average, over three and a half hours per day indoors gazing at the screens of computers, iPads and smartphones in an incessant pursuit of communication and contact with others via Zoom, WhatsApp, social media, text or plain old-fashioned email.

Some of this 'screen-time' probably makes sense, especially the ordering of vital supplies from supermarkets and the like. So much of it, however, to this cynical, moaning dinosaur-like and assuredly anti-social old toad, seems pointless – even gratuitous.

William Davies was advocating, for we inhabitants of this stressful and problem laden world, the relief of many of our tensions and worries by communing 'in person' (not virtually) with nature.

I accept that if one dwells in a conurbation such relief is not easy to find, although most cities throughout our 'sceptred isles' are reasonably well blessed with parks and open spaces. In contrast, living here as we do in the very rural, scenic South West peninsula, the opportunities to be in the fresh air and to soak up the natural beauty and serenity about us, even during the 'once a day' outdoor exercise regimen at the height of the depressing lock-down, have been on hand – and are to be coveted.

Ann and I have spent countless hours in our garden during the past 15 months. Generally it has been most relaxing, even comforting, as we have charted the changing seasons surrounded by an abundance of colourful flowers and shrubs thanks to Ann's horticultural skills and diligence; also we have had sight of – and heard the chorus (not just at dawn) of a multitude of birds of widely varying species. We have viewed squirrels practising their stunning acrobatics in the trees and on the telephone wires and even seen a hedgehog – an all too rare sight in these times.

Granted not all folk are as fortunate as us; many do not possess an outdoor space to call their own. Yet that granite, tor strewn plateau, Dartmoor, is close at hand for so many. There, to use the descriptive gem of William Wordsworth, one can 'wander lonely as a cloud'. Also, here in the South West, as the country tapers to a point at Land's End, nobody is located very far from the coast. At any time surely it is possible to gain inner peace, plus a feeling of well-being, standing on a cliff watching on a sunny day the sparkling seas running onto beaches, or in stormy weather, tempestuous waves thundering onto implacable rocks.

Still, each to his or her own, as goes the saying. As to myself, being basically of an idle disposition, I will continue to stand and stare – sit, to be more accurate – something I had perfected long before Covid-19 came along.

10

Firefighting

*I*T was a headline in a recent *Tavistock Times/Gazette* which brought back the memories: 'Cattle freed from slurry pit' it stated in bold fashion. As the saying goes – 'been there, done that and got the t-shirt'. Mind you, a filthy, very smelly shirt it was; the fact is, though, that during my eight or so years as a retained firefighter, based in Tavistock, the hub of a large rural farming area, such calls were not that uncommon; and always they were to be dreaded.

It was difficult enough – even dangerous at times – to extract a large, terrified bovine from its dung-laden bath, but that, in reality, no matter how long it took, was almost the easy part. For once the fire and rescue appliance returned to base, hours – literally – of cleansing of the fire engine and equipment took place; then as soon as one arrived home, a washing machine was abused in the pursuance of clean – and odour free – 'togs' whilst a long stint under the shower using copious amounts of soap neutralised most of the farmyard influence.

Mind you, in my early years as a fireman (the correct description then as all firefighting personnel were male) I was not involved in any farmyard calamities; for in the early

Another fine mess for Fireman Sherrell!

1960s I served for two years as a full time fireman in Plymouth before my inherent wanderlust, plus the fact I knew I did not wish to do the job permanently, caused me to leave and seek my fortune elsewhere (not that I have ever found it).

Being in the service in the 'Ocean City' was a very different experience from that which came my way in the 'old stannary town' and the wide open spaces which surround it. For the city produced the incidents one would associate with a large urban area. House blazes, often in vulnerable high rise flats, chimney fires, cars set alight, so often deliberately, automatic alarms causing attendance at department stores – at times activated by real smoke and flames – road accidents and so very much more.

In many ways though, the men I served with were vastly more interesting than the work; for so many of them were middle-aged gents nearing their retirement 'old sweats' who had joined the wartime auxiliary fire service and had endured the holocaust that was the Plymouth blitz. We younger men in the service knew that they had fought fires the like of which we would never see; generally they were unconventional, often cynical men of great practicality and courage to whom the official manuals and rule books meant nothing; often this included the officers.

Well do I remember a 'shout' we attended late of a summer evening; someone reported that there was a lot of grass on fire in a local park; everything being very dry, we hastened forth. On arrival it was discovered that the area in flames was about the size of a modest coffee table. The gnarled veteran in charge was disgusted we had been called out for something as trivial; 'I could urinate and put this lot out,' he rasped (although he did not use the word urinate). He then proceeded to do just that. When asked what message should be sent back to the control room – which was standard procedure – he snapped, 'hose reel in use'.

Those two years will remain with me always as will the period from the mid 1970s to early '80s I spent in the retained service here in West Devon. I was privileged to man appliances with some of the finest people I've ever known. Folk whose regular employment was diverse; thus each brought background knowledge which often was crucial in times of emergency – and the whole purpose of the service is to confront potential calamity.

Even though it is going on 40 years since I left, my memories of the massive range of incidents and emergencies we attended remain vivid, especially the unusual, such as the rescuing of a small dog from a rabbit hole, likewise cats from trees (several), plus the 'back breaking' such as hay and straw barn infernos, moorland blazes, removal of a boy's head from railings – without severing it, one must add; a multitude of false alarms (many malicious) also come to mind.

I have much pride in the fact that other members of our family have been in the local retained service – son James and daughter-in-law Penny, whilst these days our grandson Tom is a most able and conscientious member; my dear late brother, Stan, served the people of the Bere Peninsula in a like capacity for many years. Mind you, I have to be honest and say I was never an asset to the profession whether full time or retained; always I lacked many of the practical abilities needed – indeed, in the crucial field of tying knots, I scarcely knew a sheepshank from a sheep tick. However, I could always be relied upon to make a good cup of tea.

11

Somewhere in Heaven Argyle are Winning

M Y father, a wise man, always advised my brothers and myself to avoid discussing politics and religion in public – probably with the family also, though he never said as much.

Assuredly with Brexit, then the calamity that is Covid-19, we have had a tsunami of politics in recent times and being of, generally, a reasonably tolerant nature, and most certainly desiring to live in peace with family, friends and colleagues of widely differing views, many strongly held, I've not the slightest intention of debating such.

Certainly we have rarely lived through more polarising, passionate times during the span of our lives – which in my instance, and of numerous others encompasses a prolific number of years.

Thus with fervour in the fields of Parliament, Government and ideology remaining high, I shall avoid voicing views and outlooks on matters of state, whether local, national or world embracing.

Not that I don't have opinions and beliefs; I assuredly

do and being a man of 'a certain age', they are unlikely to alter now.

As to religion, this is possibly an even more contentious subject and a more dangerous one than the world of politics. For no matter how savage debate and disagreements become regarding the governing of our nation, mercifully it creates, here in Britain, few acts of violence.

Regrettably the same cannot be said of religion where fundamentalism and hideous intolerance all too often brings mayhem and massacre to our streets, evil terrorists killing and maiming innocent people in cold blood.

Personally, all I will say regarding my own religious persuasions is that I was raised in a good Christian home by parents who always lived by the essential tenets of Christianity.

I've attempted, all too often unsuccessfully, to live by such. However, whilst I do not intend to seek to analyse or discuss the potentially explosive minefield that can be adherence to religious belief – especially if followed zealously – I would like to talk of faith.

This, of course, covers not only spiritual belief, but a great deal more.

In this direction mine is widespread and unshakeable. I have faith in my wonderful wife, Ann, and my adored family, to always be there for me in the future as they have perpetually been in the past – and as I will ever be there for them.

I have faith (though it is not always easy) in the governmental and legal systems of our nation – plus our unique constitutional monarchy – to rule and administer with justice and respect for the common good.

The reality that, no matter how turbulent the times, civil disorder remains rare, is testimony to the fact the vast majority of we British feel likewise.

I have faith that our public services, no matter what the demands on them, will always be there for us – the NHS, fire and rescue, the police and suchlike.

Also, despite all the grim happenings in the world, I retain a faith in human nature; granted there are evil men and women who are soused in malevolence, but overwhelmingly folk are decent, honest and respectful of others.

I even have faith, despite the fact that it has been battered and abused throughout my lifetime, that Plymouth Argyle will one day be truly successful – a powerhouse in the world of football. Mind you, in this direction, I have little faith it will happen in my lifetime.

Old moaning man though I am, and will continue to be, I do not lack faith in the generations represented by my children, grandchildren and beyond; it has probably ever been the case that older folk look upon the young with concern, even despair, at the way they live their lives; surely there is no need, for that's the way the parents of we elderly looked upon us – generally unfairly.

Then, of course, there is probably the ultimate faith – that which cannot be divorced from religion.

It is one which I find becomes ever more relevant. For I am at an age now when, inevitably, the Grim Reaper will be closing in, scythe in hand.

With this in mind, I feel fortunate in the fact my faith is such – I believe in an afterlife; when my eyes close for the final time, I do not consider it will be the end; rather I believe I will move on to another world.

Where it will be, mind you, and what it will be like, clearly I have no idea. It could perhaps be heaven – but there is a fair chance it might be hell.

If it's the latter, it might well be that there is a 'next world' Football League with the Pilgrims as members. That indeed world be purgatory.

c

12

Sponsors & Sport

*I*T caught my eye when recently I was scanning the news pages devoted to local sport – a report of a football side playing in the bizarrely named, 'Earthbound Electrical Cornwall League'. This, of course, has to be better than one beginning, 'Heaven bound'; after all, nobody would wish to play in a team made up of the recently deceased (although it might bring new meaning to the term 'ghosting in at the far post').

This idle musing set off in me a chain of thought and a realisation of just how much team sports rely on sponsorship to ease financial constraints – indeed, to keep them going during these parlous times exacerbated by Covid-19.

In the same edition of the weekly there were reports of teams competing in the 'Torbay Clearance Service SDFL Tournament', the 'T20 Kernow Crash League' (cricket, although it sounds like stock car racing), the 'Clive Rosevear East Cornwall Premier League Cup' and the 'Manor Building Company Premier Division Cup'. Vastly different this from the days of my youth when local football and cricket clubs alike plied their trade, on the whole, in the simply entitled, 'Plymouth and District League, Divisions one to four'.

Nowadays, however, it is not only leagues and cup competitions that receive sponsorship, for there can be relatively few football clubs, at all levels, who do not have the name of a benefactor emblazoned upon the front of their shirts.

There is, I'm led to believe, a village football team in North Devon which has printed upon the chest of their shirts the name of the local funeral directors; in black, mind you, so tastefully done.

In the professional game virtually every club in the land are sponsored in many directions, team shirts being the most obvious. Plymouth Argyle have, for many years now, been backed quite considerably by the nation's best known and prized pasty makers; indeed, one of the most successful companies based on the South West peninsula.

Rumour has it that every contracted player has, before every fixture, to consume at least a couple of the company's pastry enclosed products – although such cynicism could be a touch inaccurate. Whatever, this vibrant company has been a good friend to The Pilgrims, especially during these virus blighted times.

One great plus with the Plymouth club, however, is that they have never adulterated the name of the stadium in which they have played for the past 118 years. It was called Home Park when they moved there in 1903 and that, in its simplicity, remains the name today. Such cannot be said of so very many other outfits. To be fair, a number of these will have moved from their original venues and will have adopted the name of the company or patron that has helped, often massively, in the creation of new stadia.

With many, though, such is not the case; they simply have cast aside long treasured titles of their homes in the pursuit of largesse. Thus the home of Stoke City, for many years patriotically named 'Britannia', is now, excruciatingly, 'The bet365 Stadium'; some nobility is restored in that it is located on 'Stanley Matthews Way', whilst there is a statue of the great man outside the ground.

Mansfield Town's 'Field Mill' abode is now the 'One Call Stadium' – a most promising appellation if one is trying to contact them, but not the most becoming of monikers for what is one of the oldest 'professional' football grounds in the world. Rochdale FC's 'Spotland' is now the 'Crown Oil Arena'; Peterborough United has renamed their 'London Road' ground as the 'Weston Homes Stadium', and so it goes on.

On a more poignant note, in 2019 Queens Park Rangers renamed their Loftus Road ground 'The Kyan Prince Foundation Stadium', after fans voted for the change in honour of their former youth team player who was fatally stabbed in 2006. A fitting tribute.

Such a revolution, of course, is not restricted to football; virtually all major sports and participants, especially if covered by television, will enjoy the patronage of sponsorship and the more successful they are, the more bountiful the rewards.

Such extends well beyond team sports; top snooker players, whilst usually being impeccably attired, will have their waistcoats festooned with small logos advertising amongst other things the likes of betting companies and breweries; darts pro's likewise; tennis stars, too, flaunt trademarks of world famous companies – many in the field of sports goods, equipment and clothing, whilst virtually all tournaments these days have their long held titles preceded by the sobriquet of their sponsor.

Clearly vast amounts of vital finance is brought into a multitude of sports at all levels by such enterprises. I, though, have no envy for those who benefit from it all, as I realise that even if I played in this age, with my inherent ineptitude it is unlikely I would be backed with sufficient funds to buy a packet of crisps.

13

Obesity

*I*T was, I believe, a Shakespearian character – possibly Sir John Falstaff – who, in a moment of sobriety and self-awareness, raged against his gross proportions; 'oh that this all too solid flesh would melt', said he – or words to that effect.

Here in Britain – a large part of the western world, in fact – there are multitudes mouthing the same thing, and numerous others who should be. For obesity – described in the Dictionary, simply, as being 'very fat' – is amongst the prime causes of so many illnesses and diseases, many bringing about early deaths; Type 2 diabetes, heart and coronary problems, strokes and the like, plus, for some, breathing problems, painful disablement regarding knee/ankle joints, digestive abnormalities, stomach ulcers and more.

I do not write of this excess of poundage in any smug, or indeed, judgemental way; assuredly I would never presume to be critical of folk carrying far more stones than is good for them (this column is ever a kilo and litre free zone); we live in a free society thus people technically have the right to consume what they like, and in the amounts they wish, as long as such substances are legal. Yet for the sake of their own health, and importantly, the concerns and fears of their loved ones, now might be the time to adjust their behaviours as it is said that in this treacherous era of Covid-19 vulnerability to this foul virus is greatly increased if one is well overweight.

Scientists have proven that a propensity for obesity is genetically hard-wired into some folk. For these unfortunate souls recognition of such is a step forward in their battle against this 'disease' and the stigma its effects can bring, but further medical advances are now required to support them in their daily struggles.

Now, I have to concede that whilst I enjoy both my food and drink – and stint on neither – I am extremely fortunate that I never seem to put on weight, no matter how much I eat, although I find with age I consume less than I used to. This partly is down to the fact that physically I am appreciably less active than previously; after all 'food is fuel', as someone once put it, succinctly and perceptively; if the 'engine' that is one's body does 'low mileage', then it will use relatively little 'petrol'. Whatever, I am built like a 'racing snake' as a friend once put it; mind you he was speaking of my shape rather than my pace – it would be a ponderous serpent indeed that could not lap me with some ease.

I was not ever thus. As a small boy, before the age of ten, I was very overweight. Not that I feasted on chocolate, crisps, biscuits and the like – this was the 1940s when all such goodies, being strictly rationed, were about as plentiful as cuckoos at Christmas. According to our GP at the time, a major contributing factor was some abnormality of the glands, but looking back, I feel it had more to do with being born and bred on a farm where there was no shortage of clotted cream, home-made butter and the like – plus the fact that my mother, a first class pasty maker, considered the creation of this sublime Westcountry savoury package to be a waste of her valuable time, unless they were more than a foot in length and the width and depth of a house brick – challenge accepted.

Becoming aware I was overweight – largely because it prevented me playing football – I went on a diet and reduced my bulk. All my life until I was about 40, however, I had to watch what I ate as the pounds accumulated with ease. Then, literally overnight, all changed. A bereavement of a loved one affected me immensely; the pounds – the stones, in fact – dropped off me; from being well overweight, I went to under where I still am.

After receiving virtually every medical examination known to mankind, it was decided that the shock of the death in the family affected my metabolism. I was destined, no matter what I consumed (within reason), to be skinny for the rest of my days. If I knew the formula for my diet and exercise free eternal slimness I could make a fortune. Sadly I have yet to figure it out.

With discipline and determination, though, excess bulk can be reduced and, ultimately, kept down to what is comfortable. In theory it is simple; eat a healthy diet with much fruit and veg, devour adequate but relatively modest portions and partake of plenty of exercise. Being in no

*'It would be a ponderous serpent indeed that
could not lap me with some ease!'*

danger of acquiring a thickening waistline myself it's easy for me to glibly put pen to paper, and I do have enormous sympathy for those who have to do little more than look at food to put on weight, as once I did. Today I'm so grateful that with my lack of willpower, I do not have to follow any such guidelines.

14

Friends & Friendship

RECENTLY I read that there was to be a reunion of the 'stars' of that famous United States sitcom Friends, which ceased production some 17 years ago. I cannot say I miss it, for never once in my life did I see it; yet it must have had much merit as it had considerable following on both sides of the Atlantic. Reading this, though, triggered in me thoughts regarding the usage and meaning of the word 'friends' and those terms associated with it.

The Dictionary describes a friend as being 'a person with whom one enjoys mutual feelings of affection and regard', and to the great majority of us the word brings to mind cherished and personal reminders of trust, kindness and shared experiences.

Use of the word does not always accord with its Dictionary definition. Such deviation can be found in the worlds of law and politics where it is used more as an expression of courtesy; in law, a barrister for the prosecution will refer to his counterpart for the defence – or vice-versa – as 'my learned friend', then proceed to attempt to de-bunk arguments put forward by that lawyer.

In politics the word is also used prolifically – but only if the man or woman is of the same political persuasion as the person speaking; in the House of Commons it will be, 'my honourable friend', in the Lords, the prefix becomes, 'noble'.

Looking to the plural, there are many groups with names proclaiming 'friendship' for a certain cause. 'Friends of the Earth' are one such organisation. In these times of climate change and chronic pollution of the natural world these 'friends' of our precious planet are committed to trying to ensure that future generations will inherit a decent, healthy and fulfilling globe in which to live.

The 'Society of Friends' is a Christian group who eschew all violence and who tread the paths of Christ in that they, possibly more than the vast majority of creeds – Christian and most others – truly 'turn the other cheek' when confronted by malevolence and dissent.

There are also 'friendly societies' – mutual aid and insurance alliances set up as non-profit organisations, there to help and bring some financial security to members of our communities who are vulnerable in terms of finance.

Also there are many entertainment and community organisations now – especially those local and lacking major financial backing – whose dedicated hard-working, fundraising supporters are known as 'friends of' whatever organisation is their particular fancy. Without their loyal benefaction, so many clubs, institutions and facilities which enhance our lives would 'go to the wall'.

In sport, especially football, there are often 'friendly

matches' – games the winning of which bring no tangible reward except the satisfaction of victory. Mind you, such contests are often far from convivial; indeed, the opposite of the cordiality conveyed in the title. I once played in such a fixture where three players were sent off for 'violent conduct'. I doubt if such would happen to anybody playing for Tonga; for this nation set in the Pacific Ocean, is known as the 'Friendly Islands'; what a delightful name for a country – one, surely, to be proud of.

During a longish life I have been so very fortunate in making many friends (some enemies, also, it must be admitted, mainly due to opinions and actions of mine when I was an elected local councillor). There remain a goodly number of these 'amigos', both male and female, that go back to my schooldays, although naturally and inevitably the numbers are constantly being reduced, ruthlessly, by the wicked scythe wielded by the 'Grim Reaper'.

In more recent times – well, the past 30 years to be precise – so many of the delightful ladies and gents I've been privileged to work with at the *Tavistock Times Gazette* I look upon as dear friends; hopefully they look upon me in the same way despite my, at times, eccentric, idiosyncratic approach to life.

I have left until last, though, my greatest, most loved comrades in this world; firstly my dear, lovely wife Ann, our four sons, plus their wives and partners in life and, also, our grandchildren plus the 'great' of that kind. They number 20 in total; all are so important to me; we are a peaceable tribe with our relationships based on mutual respect – plus, crucially, love.

Not all friendships last, however – Boris Johnson and Dominic Cummings are proof of this. Also there can be a side to it fuelled by self-interest; an example of this were the words of Sir Winston Churchill back in the war. When told that Nazi Germany had invaded the communist Soviet Union, a totalitarian state and doctrine which the great wartime Prime Minister loathed, he nonetheless declared that the tyrannical Joseph Stalin and his vast country were allies of Britain, saying, memorably, 'our enemy's enemy is our friend'.

15

Grasp the Thorn

RECENTLY I read, for the first time, evocative, mind concentrating, yet elegant words penned by that famed 19th century novelist, Ann Bronte: 'If you will not grasp the thorn, then do not crave the rose.' For a while I sat almost in awe, savouring the insightful brilliance as well as the beauty of this sentence. Sadly, however, all too rapidly, my innate, eternal, automatic cynicism gained control. I analysed what she was saying and came to the conclusion that her basic meaning was vastly more prosaic; in present day jargon she was possibly intimating that there is no such thing as a 'free lunch'.

Mind you, it can be articulated in a somewhat more upbeat, constructive way by quoting the determined motto of that elite British fighting force, the SAS 'Who Dares Wins'. Another noble expression which eschews any notion of 'something for nothing' is 'Fortune Favours the Brave'. During the early part of the Second World War, when Britain was facing the very real prospect of invasion and ultimate defeat by Nazi Germany, Sir Winston Churchill exhorted the people of our great nation to resist

– to fight and defeat this vile enemy. However, he made no secret of what the cost to citizens would be if victory, eventually, was to be achieved – the shedding of blood, toil, tears and sweat.'

The writer and philosopher, Goethe, gave the sound advice that if a person wished to progress, it was no good sitting back hoping for the best; rather he implored them to 'seize this very minute; what you can do, or dream you can, begin it; boldness has genius, power and magic in it.'

In a well known hymn it is put with passion that one should be valiant, certainly in the face of disaster; known as To be a Pilgrim, it is highly relevant regarding the stoicism and acceptance of pain required of Plymouth Argyle supporters.

In his poem, 'If' – possibly the most quoted in English literature – Rudyard Kipling lists a multitude of trials and tests which, in life, can confront a man (no doubt he would have included women also), suggesting that if their lives are to be successful and fulfilling, these have to be faced with courage, character, resilience and fortitude.

On the political front, the shameful denial of the vote to women would probably have gone on for many decades longer were it not for the Suffrage Movement – people willing to pay the price of going to prison for their beliefs.

In the United States, the oppression of the black population was eased to a degree by the leadership of Doctor Martin Luther King who inspired them to resist, peacefully, the toxic, discriminatory laws which shackled them. Assuredly there was no 'free lunch' there, as this great man paid the supreme price – assassination.

A fellow with personal ambitions was W S Gilbert and he had his ideas as to how to achieve them. He wrote, 'if you wish in this world to advance, your merits you're bound to enhance, you must stir it and stump it and blow your own trumpet or, trust me, you haven't a chance.' It certainly worked for him, he being the acclaimed lyricist of the Gilbert and Sullivan team though clearly he was much aided by his immense talent.

On a lighter note, more in keeping with Anne Bronte's observation regarding love, is the advice to suitors 'faint heart never won fair lady'. There is, though, a more serious side to this; here we talk of marriage and long term relationships. So many men and women form a union which they probably feel will last until 'death do them part'; yet, often within a few years the bond is broken, frequently causing distress and disillusion. Naturally there can be many reasons for this, but often, one feels, it can be that the 'thorns' which can pierce the harmony of a man and woman living together, are not grasped – thus the 'rose' perishes. However, if there is mutual love and respect, tolerance and a sense of duty, then surely there are few problems in matrimony which cannot be overcome.

Such was brought home to me many years ago when, as an insurance agent, I used to call on an elderly couple living locally. The lady of the house had suffered a quite severe stroke; she was cared for by her husband, himself not in the best of health. A truly good loving gentleman, his devotion to her was exemplary. So impressed was I, one day I complimented him upon it.

His reply I shall never forget; he looked at me with a facial expression of disbelief, then said, 'but my dear fellow, it is my privilege'. Assuredly he had grasped the 'thorn' and coveted the 'rose'.

16

Budapest

*A*NN and I are blessed with four fine sons. None of them now are youngsters, of course, but throughout their lives they have shown kindness, courtesy and thought for others – elderly parents are assuredly included.

This extends to holidays, where often one or other will plan a few days beyond our shores and invite us to join them. The vital aspect of this is that they will organise it all – travel arrangements, hotels and the like, currencies; with the latter, they will ever peruse the internet to find the best rate of exchange.

Thus the most onerous matter for ourselves is to pack cases and bags.

Even in this direction, my involvement is minimal, for Ann decides what we need to take, leaving me merely to pack ablution gear, electric razor and a book for bedtime reading.

Such was the situation back in July, when offspring Dave, along with his delightful partner, Rachel, invited us to go with them to Budapest for a few days; our grateful acceptance was instantaneous. Thus a hot Saturday morning found the lour of us at Luton Airport – both the town and the flying facility new to this older couple.

As usually happens when travelling to most of Europe, the convoluted, arcane assault course which confronts the hapless holiday maker when trying to get from 'check-in' onto the actual plane is vastly more fraught and lengthy than the flight itself – that being under two hours.

We flew courtesy of a Hungarian airline known as 'Wizzair', which sounded like something out of *'Harry Potter'*.

The flight posed no problems except the voices coming over the intercom system seemed strangulated and were incomprehensible. As nobody moved throughout the duration one can only assume there was no command to abandon ship.

A taxi at the other end took us to our hotel in the middle of the city, about a quarter mile from the famed River Danube; this magnificent waterway cuts the city in half, with 'Buda' on one side and 'Pest' (where we were) the other.

We had left England in a heatwave and arrived to find the 'Magyars' homeland even hotter.

The hotel lobby was awash with refreshing air conditioning; also it had abundant free supplies of tea, coffee and cold drinks (sadly non-alcoholic) until 5pm. A glance at the watch – 4.55pm – Usain Bolt could not have moved quicker.

Hungary is a smallish, scenic, land-locked country in Eastern Europe with a long, often turbulent, history.

Situated with Germany to the west and Russia to the east, those twin and, all too often, vicious giants have over the centuries (notably the twentieth) made life hell for the Magyars.

The Nazis in the 1930s and early 40s and Stalinist Soviet Union from 1945 until Glasnost in 1989, brutalised the inhabitants of this historic state – officially, in the pursuit of ideology, though clearly the prizes brought by conquest and power were greater motivators.

A museum marking this terror was very much on our itinerary, as was a visit to the magnificent Royal Palace, the Parliament Building and a leisurely trip on the Danube.

Also crucial to a relaxing, fulfilling holiday were the frequent visits we made to the multitudinous cafés and bars which dwelt in virtually every street. Sitting under an awning, on a warm summer's day, imbibing cool white wine was not a chore.

Then there is the statuary; never have I witnessed as much. It is as if long ago the authorities went to a factory creating such and bought their entire, very varied stock.

Religious icons abound – Catholic, Orthodox and Protestant alike, plus the occasional Muslim contribution.

Mighty stone lions (many crushing serpents) were scattered like confetti, numerous gods and goddesses (some ridiculously scantily clad for a country which has cold winters) proliferated, national leaders, heroes and soldiers of past times gazed outwards and upwards from their plinths.

Mind you, seeing as their country was so often in bondage, one has to question their competence in defending it.

Sadly, good things come to an end – rapidly. Thus did a hot Tuesday afternoon see us, reluctantly, check out of our cool, comfortable hotel.

My mind was prey to the dismal realisation that sumptuous breakfasts would cease.

Now it's strange how appetites can be linked to finance. At home this early meal is meagre – at times ignored altogether; in the hotel, where it was already paid for, I put away a full English plus a decent Continental – and seconds.

'Set up for the day', as they say! As to the aforementioned currency, the Magyars use the little known Forint. I knew better than to cause panic in local banks by asking for those.

17

Presenters

No person I know of either gender has a greater love of sport than my wife, Ann.

She has considerable knowledge, so often understanding tactics and finer points which pass me by even though I have a fairly wide interest myself in these pursuits.

Cricket, rugby (both codes), tennis, snooker and football all grab her attention – if she is not busy – when on television. Indeed, she is not averse to spectating at live sport on occasions, quite often showing character traits of the highest order by going to Home Park.

Emotionally, watching Argyle can be extremely draining (well it is to me); however, while noisy with, it has to be conceded, the odd profane word bellowed from the stands, it has a distinct advantage over TV coverage – there is no commentary.

This was brought home to me a while back when Ann was watching the French Open tennis tournament; though there was no sound, for she had pushed the mute button.

She was suffering a little in this silence, for she quite enjoys the atmosphere created by a crowd engrossed in a sport, as do I. What she could not stand however – understandably – was the constant yap from the presenters, worst of whom was Jim Courier (if there has to be comment, at least let it come from the lips of a Briton).

The real point is, though, that the great plus with TV is it is a visual medium; few words are ever needed because one can see exactly what's happening.

Still, the viewer, with judicial use of the mute button, can usually have a reasonably satisfying time as, mostly, cameras do show sporting action, whether on court, pitch, wicket, table or race track.

If only that were true of activities at other events, some iconic, covered by BBC and ITV alike. Being a lover of flowers and colourful gardens (well stocked kitchen plots plus shows of prize vegetables also have allure), I looked forward to coverage of the most famous show dedicated to such – Chelsea.

Thus, Ann and I settled down one evening to view an hour's programme about this annual event. For her, the gardener of the family, it was about enjoying the sight of the most perfect flowers and veg the world has to offer, plus the hope of picking up the odd tip or two – for me it was just the pleasure to be derived from absorbing the sight of flora grown almost to perfection. We were to be disappointed.

The first part of the telecast was dominated by the presenters – whose inane chatter would have been too daft for Monty Python's Flying Circus – interviewing 'celebrities', only one of whom we had heard of.

It was clear that most of them were there because they probably got in for nothing and knew they would be invited to stand before the cameras. Many gave the impression they scarcely knew the difference between a rose and Japanese knotweed.

About half way through, our spirits were lifted – we were to be shown some gardens. Despondency descended rapidly, for most of these show pieces (some of which must have been funded by Russian oligarchs, so ornate were they) owed far more to Avantgarde architects and sophisticated builders than to gardeners, foliage and flowers being about as plentiful as diamonds in a slurry pit.

The programme ended with presenters being even more annoying – and never a sign of the flower or produce tent.

Coverage of Crufts was little better. Here in the land which is home (probably) to the world's greatest dog lovers, hours of viewing time is rightly devoted to the most iconic canine show in the world, where the winning of rosettes make the recipients literally 'top dogs' universally.

Sadly little animal life was to be seen. Talk though, abounded, with tedious commentators so often exuding synthetic, excessive enthusiasm, endlessly chatting to the inevitable 'celebs', many seemingly with little knowledge of hounds and probably even less interest.

To be fair, the occasional dog would appear, but usually chasing around some pointless assault course, to pretentious delight from dreary presenters. Fleeting glimpses of champion breeds were to be seen – but it was vital not to blink.

Likewise with the dancing in BBC's Strictly Come Dancing. We've ceased to watch it – originally it was dedicated to the fine (or at times, leaden) footwork of the contestants, but now it seems dominated by prattling pundits and 'prima donna' judges. Any viewer taking longer than five minutes to make a cup of tea would miss the ballroom action almost in its entirety. It could be said that the old silent films had much merit.

d

18

In the Hands of Medics

*A*S there is little danger of me being brutalised by a vicious thug or slain by a hired assassin, it cannot be remotely equated with being in the hands of the mafia.

Yet, at present, my life is not entirely my own and to a degree I am not sure it ever will be again, for I have fallen in thrall to the medical profession. At my age it could be I will never escape. Life at the moment, though still sweet and well worth the living, is punctuated by summons to visit medics and hospital to consult doctors and specialists and partake in more tests than the England cricket team will in a decade.

Not that there is much wrong with me – and what there is can be explained largely by the fact that my aged body (and mind) is slowly wearing out – inevitable with we mortals. A while back I had one or two problems – relatively mild – for which I felt it only wise to seek medical advice, the 'stitch in time' philosophy coming to the fore. I'm not sure I should have heeded such thoughts. Whatever, a few months back I made an appointment to see my GP. Feeling my demise was not imminent, I agreed to the excessive three weeks delay before I could see the doctor with whom I am registered. The day duly arrived, so I, still blessed with a pulse, took myself off to the surgery.

'You're next on,' the charming receptionist reassured, so I took a seat. I was not tempted to peruse any of the somewhat bland, and much thumbed, magazines which proliferated as I anticipated my name being called within minutes. In actual fact I could have read the bulk of *War and Peace* by the time I was hailed.

There was no operating table in the doctor's sanctum, which surprised me as he had clearly spent so long with his previous patient he could well have been performing heart surgery. Still, I was in and the physician, a most attentive gent, invited me to speak of that which ailed me. He listened, asked a few questions, checked my blood pressure (which was tolerably low as I'd not been to Home Park for a while), then with a serious expression on his face informed me that a scan would be advisable and he would arrange it. Where would it be carried out, I enquired? His one word response would have struck terror in the heart of a Victoria Cross hero – Derriford.

The 'Dunkirk Spirit' was marshalled and some couple of months later (this was classed as an urgent appointment), the journey made to the mammoth hospital on the edge of the great 'Ocean City'.

Although there is an excellent bus service, I decided to drive – not wise. My stress levels when approaching the medical 'Leviathan' were reasonably low; however, by the time I had parked the car, they were close to causing a coronary. Firstly, one had to queue for entry. When eventually the barrier was reached, there were instructions to read and buttons to press which, to an idiot like me, were largely incomprehensible. Eventually a blue disc popped from a slot and the barrier lifted.

I then found myself trundling around the huge car park in ever decreasing circles searching for a space – at last, one was found. Close by was a sign which informed of parking charges. I was outraged; my vehicle was not parked, rather it was being held to ransom.

The hospital was entered; being vast, I wandered its multitudinous corridors for what seemed hours and was close to a breakdown before at last locating the venue I needed.

A few days later a phone call summoned me into the presence of my GP – my results had arrived.

His greeting on entering his consulting room did not elevate my confidence in him, nice fellow though he is, for his first words were an enquiry 'What can I do for you?' I pointed out I was there, at his behest, under the assumption he was now aware of what was ailing me. Annoyingly he did not know – my hospital visit had been of no help in terms of diagnosis. Thus during the next few months there were many more tests, X-rays and scans. Enough blood was siphoned from my veins to sustain a rampant Dracula for months.

Has diagnostic progress been made? No – tests remain ongoing. Despite this though, I'm told that a visit from the 'Grim Reaper' is not expected in the short term; I could be around for several football seasons yet. Mind you, I'm not sure such is an inducement towards seeking longevity.

19

Gardening

'*H*OW many kinds of sweet flowers grow in an English country garden? I'll tell you now of some that I know and those I miss you'll surely pardon.'

So goes the words of a delightful, well known song extolling the virtues of the myriad flora to be found in so many of the outside spaces throughout our islands.

My wife, Ann, a good, knowledgeable gardener, will be able to name virtually all in the plot surrounding our house, and the vast majority in those of others.

To my shame, I can name very few. It's not that I do not like vibrant colour surrounding our home – indeed, the sun shining on vividly hued blooms and subtly shaded shrubs, complemented by an emerald green lawn (though it must be conceded that in our verdant strip, moss contributes much to such a colour) never fails to bring me pleasure and a certain relaxed peace of mind.

The identity of such, however – except for the obvious such as roses, snowdrops, rhododendrons and the like, are well beyond me.

This puzzles Ann; she points out that I am a farmer's

son, a member of a clan that has been working the land for generations. So how, she wonders, am I so ignorant when it comes to that which comes from the soil?

The answer is simple and applies to many with an agricultural background, active farmers as well for that matter – folk who earn their living harvesting the bounty which comes from the earth, produce principally that which can be eaten rather than looked at.

Mind you, my parents being as much horticulturists as farmers, did grow flowers – up to a dozen acres of daffodils in springtime, and a sizeable area of anemones for gathering in late autumn and early winter. These, though, were not raised for their undeniable beauty, but were cash crops; when picked, they were despatched by train (prior to Doctor Beeching) to the far corners of the kingdom.

The garden around our farmhouse (if I recall correctly) had a few nondescript shrubs and a couple of chicken coops, the residents of which – the sturdy Rhode Island Red – produced ample eggs for our dietary needs.

To be fair, then and now, some workers of the land would have blooms and attractive foliage around their dwellings, but the majority, if they had anything at all, would probably settle for spuds usefully close to the kitchen when needed to give backbone to their Sunday roast.

So having said this, the question could fairly be asked as to why I've not turned at least a small part of our reasonably sized patch into a kitchen garden. The answer is that I did, at Ann's suggestion, try to do so a few years back. She greatly overestimating my competence, left me to it. Potatoes, carrots, cabbages, onions and so forth were tilled (with more hope than expectation, it has to be said) and harvest time awaited. Sadly, the planting took infinitely longer than the reaping, for due to a grievous combination on my part of failure to feed the soil and spray for the multitude of ravenous pests which decimated what little crop there was (plus a far too tolerant attitude towards weeds), that which I gleaned would not have filled the belly of an undersized rabbit.

Vegetable growing was abandoned. For many years now, my gardening activities have been limited in scope – mowing lawns and labouring under the guidance of Ann who assuredly knows what she is doing when it comes to the nurturing of the beautiful vision a garden can produce. Early in our marriage she realised my knowledge of such was abysmal; for I treasured most carefully a fine looking plant which turned out to be a weed, whilst carting off to the dump a shrub (to my eye, quite nondescript) which had been bought, not cheaply, from a garden centre.

Mind you, I am not complaining when it comes to having had, long ago, arboricultural responsibilities lifted from my shoulders. I'm quite happy to potter about in warm sunshine and fresh air with someone else making the decisions.

Having said this, I'm far more gratified when able to sit on the patio, enjoy the 'great outdoors' and sip from a glass awash with an alcoholic beverage.

There is though a problem; for the vagaries of British weather means, so often, the periods one can sit and relax in one's outside plot can be quite rare, and when they come, have to be dedicated to tidying and maintenance.

So the question has to be asked as to why God, to whom so much credit is given for natural beauty, does so little towards keeping it tidy and eliminating the weeds?

20

Bah Humbug

*I*T has been in my mind for some time that being a grumpy, miserable old toad, I could possibly put together a handbook of tips regarding (in my view) the preparations which those with a touch of Ebeneezer Scrooge about us, should make if we are to survive the upcoming tidal wave of terrifying jollity and good will.

The Yuletide is just days hence. Some folk will have made few arrangements – in some instances because they find the hectic, chaotic, even stress-laden week or so before the big day a time of fun, excitement, adrenalin pumping action.

To be prepared for it would, to them, take away so much of the joy of this annual celebration. Most though who are unready for the jollifications enter the period immediately prior to Santa's coming in a state of panic because they simply have put off, until virtually the last minute, getting organised for it.

The curmudgeon, he (occasionally she), viewing the festive season as being a couple of weeks to survive with a minimum of expenditure and association with one's fellow man and woman – but who has no desire to offend – surely dare not leave things to the last minute.

Indeed, plans need to be made long before – during the previous Christmas in fact. To be more exact, Boxing Day.

For then, when liquor abused heads (well, mine will be) have cleared a little, a list should be made of all gifts received, and from whom; the relevant ones here are those which we do not want – gadgets we will never use, clothes which will not be worn and the like. Such items, of course, are far too good to throw away.

Now some folk will be very ungracious, almost brutal, in fact. Often within a week or so of having received the gift, they will advertise the item for sale in the bargain ads of their local paper and describe it with chilling honesty as being an unwanted present.

Part of the entry will be a contact phone number, thus the identity of the ungrateful recipient can easily be discerned by one and all, including the giver.

Some more conscientious folk may well deliver such to a charity shop, but a third way, one which can save a few bob, is to pass on articles to family and friends with a fresh piece of gift wrap the following December – or even the one after that.

Thus the importance of registering the original bestower of such objects – it will assuredly not strengthen friendships or family ties to send the unloved offering to the original donor.

Done correctly, though, it can ease pressure on the pocket and in this environmentally conscious era, be classed as recycling.

A record should also be kept of cards received, for if

one is not sent greetings this year then the miscreant should be struck from the sending list for next – money would be saved.

As to the purchasing of such, this should also be done on Boxing Day when retailers are shifting unsold stock at radically reduced rates.

Likewise, presents should always be bought in sales and preferably early in the year to avoid anxiety later.

The only small minus here is that the person for whom a certain gift was intended might in the meantime be harvested by the Grim Reaper. This, however, is unlikely and even if it does occur, then another home for it can easily be found.

Then there is the social side of matters; parties, family do's, get-togethers, all a daunting, almost frightening tsunami of jollity and bonhomie.

To avoid such, plausible excuses which will not offend should be catalogued in the mind of we misanthropes well before the season.

Mind you, exceptions can be made for celebrations where free alcohol might well flow faster than the Tavy.

Having stated such a jaundiced view and approach regarding Christmas, a fair question would be as to whether or not I keep to it.

An honest answer is – no. My 'bah humbug' attitude is more than neutralised by Ann. She enjoys the festive period, prefers giving to receiving, loves to see as many family and friends as possible and does virtually all the work and preparations towards it, including the cooking at which she is superb.

There is though, possibly, a debit side to this, for it tends to undermine this grumbling old man as it dissuades me from penning my cynic's guide (a potential best seller?), for while I feel there is an argument in favour of my aforementioned approach, the generosity and positivity of my dear spouse erodes it.

Indeed, I have to admit, somewhat shamefacedly, that when the Yuletide finally arrives – I actually love it.

A Happy Christmas to one and all.

21

Figuring it Out

ANY claim that our lives – indeed, the world in general – is influenced greatly by 'lies, damned lies and statistics'. Assuredly numerous, at best gross exaggerations, at worst total untruths, permeate our existence, influence our thoughts plus the way we live our lives and we are not always aware of them. Some are reasonably apparent, others far less so; a shrewd, calculating malcontent using, say, social media, will be adept at spreading lies in such a subtle way that such are accepted as being factual.

Statistics, though, are somewhat different; for these are very rarely figures adjusted in a false way; indeed usually they are completely accurate. Yet unless measured against the yardstick of logic and common sense, they can be irrelevant, time wasting and plain foolish. Never, to my mind, was this more clearly exemplified than at a gathering many years ago when I was privileged to sit as a magistrate on the West Devon Bench, which was made up of JPs from the Tavistock and Okehampton areas. We were summoned by the clerk to the court to attend an emergency meeting at the Courthouse in the 'Old Stannary Town'. Clearly, it was, we all assumed, a crucial matter which needed urgent attention.

We assembled, some 20 of us, in the fine old Victorian building (now, at last, being restored), on a chilly mid winter afternoon. The clerk – the solicitor in charge of all court proceedings – thanked us for our attendance. He then apologised for the short notice given regarding our assembly but stressed he was only following orders from the Home Office; it appeared we had transgressed; we had as a Bench contravened guidelines – if not rules – laid down by Government lawyers and advisors based at Westminster.

'It seems,' said the clerk, his facial expression that of a man suffering intense embarrassment, 'that this court is, before trial, remanding in custody far too high a percentage of people charged with grievous bodily harm. Unless it is a brutal attack and the alleged perpetrator could be a danger to the public, the policy is to remand on bail. The desire of the Home Office is for fewer than 20% of defendants to be imprisoned awaiting trial. Unfortunately this Bench has remanded, in custody, 50% of those who have come before them this past year charged with GBH.'

Perplexity abounded. 'I wasn't aware we were particularly draconian in that direction,' the Bench chairman stated in somewhat bewildered fashion. 'We just do what we feel to be right. Anyway, what numbers are we talking of here – how many have been denied bail?'

The clerk gazed fixedly at the far wall, then took a deep breath; 'Well, during this period we had,' – he stopped and cleared his throat; 'we had two charged with GBH and refused bail for one; so technically the Home Office is correct – 50% have been remanded to prison.'

Was there ever a greater example of a statistic, though accurate, which abused common sense. Mind you, in so many other directions statisticians bring forth facts that, though accurate, can confuse, mislead and often state the obvious. An example of the latter was a recent news item which stated that surveys showed, statistically, that folk who smoked, drank and over ate. generally had a shorter life expectancy than those with a healthy lifestyle; really? Well, there's a surprise. Another report was that statistics proved that those with a university degree were likely to earn more than those without; this is a situation often unfair, but not exactly a stunning revelation.

So far this has been a somewhat dismissive attack on the value and point of statistics; but it is time to put forward a positive side to them. To be fair, there are some, probably none more than those dedicated to the contentious debate over what is the supreme challenge confronting the world – climate change. In this the 'S' word reigns supreme, for it shows, factually and without opinion, just how much temperatures, worldwide, are rising and offers, in a totally neutral way, a warning to us all.

Fortunately, it would appear to be heeded. It is to be hoped it is not too late. Mind you, whilst acknowledging the immense seriousness of such, I have to confess that the stats to which I pay most attention are those printed in a league table beside the title Plymouth Argyle; if good, they bring joy, if bad, desolation.

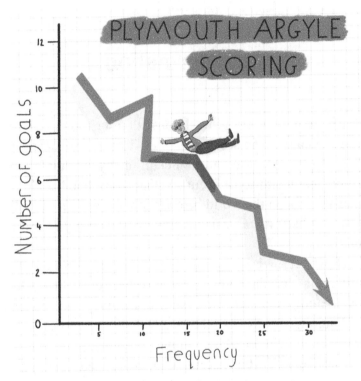

*Oh dear, looks like the Plymouth Argyle
statistics are plummeting again!*

22

Misinformation

WE live in an era of misinformation, or to put it more bluntly – and accurately – lies. This, to an extent, has ever been the case; a politician, many decades ago, commented with some accuracy, that a falsehood could be 'halfway round the world before truth had got out of bed'; and way back it was stated that the first casualty of war is fact.

However, whilst such deviation has existed for millennia (propaganda is little other than this), the frightening sophistication and immediacy of modern technology means that the malevolent can afflict, even terrorise, at will, at whim and instantaneously.

The likes of Twitter, Facebook and social media in general, can be welcome avenues for dispatching information and news worldwide of an honest, positive nature, doing so instantly; but in the hands of the perverse, malcontents and bullies, it can cause hurt, harm and misery. Sadly it would appear to be a price extracted from society in what is termed progress. In numerous ways, instant communication has many benefits; however, is it a price worth paying?

Mind you, throughout history folk have been reported as making statements, often of a derogatory nature, which subsequently they have denied ever uttering. An example – Sir Winston Churchill supposedly said of his principal political opponent, Clement Attlee, that he was 'a modest man with plenty to be modest about'; the great wartime leader denied saying it.

Likewise Napoleon claimed he never called the British 'a nation of shopkeepers', and it is surely most unlikely than immediately prior to the French Revolution, Queen Marie Antoinette, when told 'the people have no bread' retorted with the banal, insensitive, 'then let them eat cake'; and, laying mortally wounded, it is virtually certain Horatio Nelson never said, 'kiss me Hardy'; 'kismet' was probably the term he used. In the last century – the 1930s as he lay terminally ill – did King George V, when encouraged by optimistic doctors that he would soon be sufficiently fit to go to the popular Bognor Regis, say 'b***** Bognor'? Doubtful, one feels.

In Hollywood in that same era – less controversially – that star of many gangster films, James Cagney, never spoke the line with which he has been eternally credited, 'you, you dirty rat – I'm going to get you.' Famed quotes from literature also are often not recalled with precision; 'alas poor Yorick, I knew him well' – Hamlet supposedly claimed such, but Shakespeare did not include 'well'; Arthur Conan Doyle, it is believed widely, had Sherlock Holmes declaiming, often, 'elementary, my dear Watson'; yet not once in his multitude of tales did he use the phrase; 'elementary' was the sole word expressed on occasions.

Then there are the legendary claims which have

transcended the centuries; did 'Nero' really 'fiddle while Rome burned', or Robert the Bruce gain inspiration to resist the English armies by watching a spider build a web – both highly unlikely; and surely Sir Francis Drake would have been far too busy marshalling his fleet prior to the imminent arrival of the Spanish Armada to contest a game of bowls on Plymouth Hoe. As to King Alfred 'burning the cakes' – nonsense, surely; and what about King Arthur's 'castle' at Tintagel; it is mystifying anybody believes he lived there, for if this possibly mythological monarch existed at all, he was never in Cornwall; the fact is, his so called castle was a monastery; and how about the Old Testament of the Bible; here one has to devour a multitude of pinches of salt to believe most of its contents.

Accepted history too is often distorted; conflict and conquest will usually be recorded with positivity and justification by the victors, the viewpoint and qualities of the vanquished generally ignored; and English Medieval History is mainly recorded by monks and priests as often they were the only people who could read and write; thus the Catholic Church almost invariably enjoyed a 'good press'.

To be fair, though, some misinformation can be down to error, at times little short of comical; several come to mind, but none possibly more bizarre than the faux pas made by President John F Kennedy when he addressed a huge crowd in Germany.

'Ich bin ein Berliner,' said he, clearly attempting to establish a rapport with the dwellers within that capital city. The problem was that, translated, what he uttered was, 'I am a doughnut'. One imagines the aide who fed him that line was rapidly consigned to the dole queue.

23

Holiday Brochures

USUALLY those hard working, most reliable ladies and gentlemen who take away our recycling handle the boxes as if they are full of feathers.

They come thundering along the pavement, often running, then almost in a single movement, hoist aloft the receptacle, empty its contents into the bowels of the monster-like lorry before hurtling on their way, the pace the same no matter what the weather, which at times can be atrocious.

Having struggled up the path with the container, this puny old man never fails to admire their strength, energy and dedication. However, there is at least one week in the year when the emptying of the box holding paper really tests them. Indeed, it would be a challenge for the mighty Anthony Joshua – and he is heavyweight champion of the world.

This happens, usually, in early February. It will contain predominantly the holiday brochures, guides and booklets which would have thudded onto our front door mat throughout January.

It will begin during the first week of the new year and carry on, probably, for most of the month at the very least.

It certainly occurred this year – nothing on January 1, of course, as it being a bank holiday, Royal Mail does not deliver, but the very next day there were two. These were followed by a regular supply for the rest of the month.

The holidays advertised are many and varied, of wide ranging cost (though few could be described as cheap) and cover a comprehensive variety of locations, some so unusual – bizarre, even – they would not ever intrude into the thought processes of most folk, myself included.

One spoke glowingly of a walking holiday in the Pyrenees, with an option for the even more hardy of a pleasant ramble in the Himalayas (one assumes oxygen cylinders would be provided). Both were roughly the purchase price of a decent car. Thus, one would pay a small fortune to have blistered feet and be permanently exhausted!

In the words of John McEnroe, they 'cannot be serious'. However, some folk clearly relish these challenges, such is the rich, divergent, idiosyncratic nature of the human race. Now prominent amongst the plethora of glossy magazines are invitations to cruise. There seems not to be a solitary ocean, sea or river from the Arctic to its equivalent in the southern hemisphere upon which one cannot sail in craft of many sizes, in varying degrees of luxury.

While not poverty stricken, seeing some of the prices quoted, Ann and I would probably have to settle for a trip to the Dogger Bank as paying passengers on a trawler out of Lowestoft or the like.

Mind you, among the multitude of seafaring adventures there was at least one quite affordable, a journey up and down some Norwegian fjords. The only problem here was that those which would be comfortable cost wise took place in December and January, when temperatures would be below zero and even more relevantly, there would probably be less than an hour's daylight in every 24.

Still, at least the ship on which we would have travelled seemed to be modestly sized, carrying hundreds of passengers rather than thousands. Some of these mighty liners have the size and populations of small towns. Being a man who could get lost in a phone box I fear I would leave my cabin and never be seen again.

It's not only invitations to take to the water which cascade through the letterbox. There is ever a super abundance of coach tours to choose from. Many are for trips to the far corners of our lovely islands. The plus here is that there will be no killing of time at tedious airports. The minus, as with all such organised holidays, is that one's itinerary is governed by the tour guide. You might spend a couple of hours at the most boring of venues, and just ten minutes somewhere you could happily pass a morning.

Being the anti-social, miserable old toad that I am, I am most unsuited to group activities. Fortunately Ann is far more tolerant of the foibles of folk – probably an explanation as to how she has put up with me for almost five decades.

There are invitations too, many of them sent out by companies who target we of more mature years, to endure long coach journeys around Europe. With our advanced age in mind, many give inducements, not least among them the pledge that if one dies in foreign parts, their insurance will cover repatriation of one's corpse.

Practical of course, but somehow off-putting. Unless invited abroad by our kindly sons, we will stick to a week or two in holiday cottages in our own lovely country – and drive there ourselves.

24

England & the World Cup

*E*XCEPT for possibly our participation in the Winter Olympics where we, as a nation, harbour few hopes, it's doubtful if in recent times any sports team has left our shores with less expectation of glory than the England football squad in early June.

Granted, the national side had qualified with relative ease, but it could be argued that dear old Plymouth Argyle might well have overcome some of the outfits in their group. Still, the saying is 'you can only beat what's in front of you', and this Gareth Southgate's players achieved.

Vladimir Putin's vast Russia was the host for the finals; not an attractive one for either sportsmen or supporters with the present political situation in mind, plus the chilling issue of innocent British subjects being murdered by, allegedly, agents from that state. Thus, when the group matches at the finals began, relatively few English fans were present (certainly compared with previous World and European Championships).

This was compounded by the general feeling that the

nation flying the flag of St George would achieve little. However, they had a decent start with victory over Tunisia. Though at times it was a little laboured, suddenly, hopes rocketed. Panama were put to the sword, 6-1.

The fact the hapless central American outfit would have struggled to overcome the average conference side was swept away amidst a tsunami of euphoria, for England had guaranteed themselves a place in the last 16 – the knock-out stage – which meant their final group fixture (and subsequent defeat) versus a very good Belgian side was of little relevance. Having retired many of the 'old guard', the England manager had gone east with a squad of young players who, between them, had probably accumulated far fewer 'caps' than would be found in the average Lowry painting.

Indeed, some of the squad struggle to get regular spots in their club sides and thus their profiles, for international footballers, is unusually low. Or, to be more accurate, it was. For victory in the first of their knock-out matches raised their image immeasurably; likewise it elevated the spirits and expectations of the nation.

Colombia had been the opposition; They were a sound bunch in terms of ability, but on the pitch they behaved with an anarchic, pre-meditated cynicism the like of which was scarcely equalled by the bandits in 'The Magnificent Seven'. But Hallelujah, for once our team won a penalty shoot out! Following this battle the English nation mobilised; flags abounded on houses and cars, pubs with large TV screens were awash with customers, as were the liquor sections of supermarkets. Newspapers, national and local, banished Brexit to the inside pages (though only temporarily, no doubt), and the slogan, 'Football's coming home' was emblazoned far and wide.

A sun drenched Saturday afternoon followed – yet beaches, streets, shops were quiet, if not deserted. The Three Lions were confronting Sweden in the quarter finals. The Scandinavian outfit were a sound side as they usually are, and assuredly more civilised than the desperados whom England had confronted in the previous round. Gloriously, on the day the 'kings of the jungle' roared in triumph, winning 2-0.

The semi-finals loomed, with Croatia the opposition. It was getting very, very exciting – and serious. So, to a sunny Wednesday evening; even more than the previous weekend, roads were virtually traffic free, all outdoor spaces exceedingly sparsely populated. Pubs, on the other hand – as long as they have screens – were thronged, with a wide range of British humanity downing copious amounts of liquor of all varieties. English flags proliferated along with a sprinkling of Union Jacks.

A heartfelt, passionate rendering of God Save The Queen had only just ceased, when England scored. Fantastic – what a start. Sadly, this was as good as it got. The opposition refused to do the decent thing and accept defeat. A side where every surname appears to end in 'ic' began to get the upper hand, especially in the second half. An experienced but ruthless outfit who would never win awards for fair play, they nevertheless had some first class players and they won. As is nearly always the case, natural British 'phlegm' exerted itself. Glasses were emptied, shoulders were shrugged and folk went to bed.

Naturally, being a patriot, I felt deeply disappointed.

e

However, I have an advantage over most other fans. For having been a foot soldier in the 'Green Army' for over 60 years, the calm acceptance of defeat for my football heroes is embedded in the DNA. I merely look forward to England's next search for glory in four years' time – assuming I'm still around.

25

Pass Me the Biro

MY parents had the phone installed when I was very young and I was brought up appreciating its value in terms of communication. So it was only natural Ann and I had one installed long ago when we moved into our first house together.

Now, those kind resilient folk who valiantly read my meanderings are probably enquiring so what? After all, the number of citizens in our great land who do not have landlines – and in these times, mobiles also, will be miniscule. The reason I state this is that, because of my terror of technology, craven approach to communication, ignorance of the internet, my DNA of a dinosaur and, to an extent, passion for privacy, I have never moved beyond the basic invention of Alexander Graham Bell back in the nineteenth century. Fortunately Ann has, in that she possesses a mobile phone though she rarely uses it. Were it not for the fact the landline phone was part of my childhood, I would possibly be terrified of even that; my sole forward movement in the field of getting messages and such to fellow human beings would probably have been to upgrade my carrier pigeon – retiring an ageing one, replacing it with a younger, faster bird. The folly of it all is that I am fully aware of my selfishness – the difficulties I cause others when they wish to have contact with me and indeed, the unnecessary barriers I put in my own path when wishing to get hold of them.

Not having a mobile, there is assuredly no texting to anyone either. To be honest, even if such advanced equipment came into my possession, I'd not have the slightest idea how to use it and even less desire (plus, in truth, courage) to learn. Instead of employing my fingers on a keypad sending letters and words through the ether, I use them to operate the sophisticated gadget I carry in my coat pocket; 'Biro' is marked upon it, and to deliver its output I employ the excellent services of a longstanding organisation known as Royal Mail. Mind you, whilst I state all this in honesty, I am not unaware of the foolishness of such cowardice.

Also, I am mindful I am a hypocrite, for whilst with friends and benevolent colleagues I play the 'old dog, new tricks' card when it comes to my cyber dread, I am rarely reticent when it comes to asking them to employ the internet for personal matters – buying tickets, booking holidays, accessing data, obtaining facts via 'Google' and the like. Indeed, I rarely now risk a hernia by lifting down from the shelves mighty tomes of the Encyclopaedia Britannica, when requiring intelligence, thanks to the patient help of others getting details up on screen; but if they did not, would I change my reactionary mode? No – it would be back to the weightlifting and the, often, difficult scanning of fine printed yellowing lines.

'I'm ready to upgrade my carrier pigeon, please.'

Mind you, whilst I concede I cause myself and others problems due to my 'Luddite' ways, I take some comfort from the fact that I can never be tempted into the minefield (certainly potentially a terrifying one, it seems to me) which can be the territory known as 'social media'. Facebook, Twitter, YouTube, the wider internet all clearly play a huge, almost dominant part in modern dialogue and human interaction; at their best their employment can bring so much benefit to the user and ease so much of the pressures of modern life. There is, though, as is so well known, very much another side, one pregnant with peril; a zone seemingly so often the terrain of the predator – those malevolents, perverts, malcontents, deviants, degenerates and just plain nasty, whose aim in life, it would appear, is to cause pain, distress, misery, often real harm to others, frequently for the sole reason it brings to them malicious pleasure and twisted satisfaction. Such is made worse by the fact that these vile individuals pursue their merciless abuse under the shield of anonymity.

Due to these cruel cowards, many lives are blighted – some ruined; indeed, there are those tragically driven to suicide. Mind you, there are some who bring troubles to their own doors, men and women alike who put comments on social media perhaps critical of others or controversial in diverse directions which can alienate colleagues, friends, even family. Indeed with politicians and celebrities, it can ruin careers. Mule headed die hard that I am, such a calamity will never come my way; nor will an annoying email; And I'll never have my rest disturbed by a mobile call or a text. Indeed, the more I think of it, this unsociable old moaner has not the slightest motive to change his Medieval ways.

26

The Nanny State

*A*S a passionate believer in democracy and personal freedom, I view with some disquiet seemingly escalating state interference in how we live our lives.

Granted, there have to be laws and regulations which curb or prevent actions and behaviour that adversely affect others, but increasingly governments appear to be involving themselves, in terms of direct legislation (or the threat of it) in how citizens pursue their own way through this world.

This is moving beyond advice or guidance – rather it's becoming intrusion, especially in health matters.

Now clearly the legislature has a duty regarding the welfare and wellbeing of the people, but one questions whether governments have any right to regulate citizens' personal habits and choices (as long as they are keeping to the laws of the land) because they feel they know what is best for folk.

It is known (accurately, one feels) as the 'nanny state'. There is a move to prevent pubs and shops selling cheap alcohol – or modestly priced, at least – because it is felt people will drink themselves into stupors unless the cost of liquor is made somewhat prohibitive. This could be true of some, but the vast majority of us can be relied on to imbibe with sufficient moderation to ensure we do not wither our livers or become enemies to public order. Such a policy would mean that to curb the few, the many will be punished.

Then there are sweets, chocolates and the like. It would appear regulations could be brought in which will instruct shops and stores where they can – and, more relatively, cannot – locate such products for sale on their own premises.

The 'powers that be' feel such is necessary because if confectionery is stacked near checkouts, it encourages children to badger their parents into buying them – products which can aid obesity and the rotting of young teeth. This can possibly be true, but surely it is unfair to traders. We, famously, were dubbed by Napoleon Bonaparte, 'A nation of shopkeepers'. In that we are an entrepreneurial, commercially minded race, it was reasonably accurate; it remains so.

For various reasons retail outlets of all sizes, stocking the widest range of products, are struggling to survive, yet it seems that 'authority' is about to make it even tougher for some, with vendors being told in effect to put their best selling lines in corners of their premises where few can locate them – including, of course, adults and responsible youngsters (the majority).

This surely is wrong. The 'rationing' of what can be unsuitable 'treats' for children (if eaten in excess) has to be down to parents. They must just say no, not that tough a word to utter. Advice – indeed warnings – come forth perpetually regarding levels of fats, salt and sugar in every day food, plus the need to avoid such.

Fair enough – those who value their fitness and health will heed such guidance – and most do, having a varied, healthy diet which can include all three of these, but in modest portions.

Can it be just that producers, retailers and the like, suffer constant interference and harassment from medical and government bodies as to what their fare should contain when most edible products are already labelled with a summary of the ingredients? This is important, of course, and sensible, but surely sufficient. The purchaser, being aware and fully informed as to what they are buying for their family and themselves, must be treated as responsible adults and permitted to decide on the suitability of the cuisine.

It is, to me, an infringement of civil liberties that such a basic entitlement as being free to spend one's money on legal goods of one's choice, is under threat.

Then there are cigarettes. Now it is only right that if smoking causes offence or harm to others it be not tolerated. Thus its banning universally from public buildings and businesses is both fair and correct. However, the use of tobacco (in the right location) is an entirely legal pursuit and, surely, should be respected as such.

I would submit, though, that it is not. Now, being a life long non-smoker, I have no axe to grind on this, but it appears to me that while governments are delighted to gain billions of pounds in taxes, yearly, from the sale of the leaf Sir Walter Raleigh brought to our shores 400 years ago, they force stores to hide tobacco in cupboards with blank, closed doors which must complicate matters for the shops and potentially give some customers, unjustifiably, a sense of guilt.

A multitude of issues, problems and, too often, calamities, confront our country. Would it not be best for one and all if Westminster confronted those and left folk to get on with their lives?

27

Superstition

RECENTLY I heard the tale of a fellow who was driving along a country road without either of his hands holding the steering wheel. In one he held the pasty he was devouring, whilst with the other he appeared to be making military style salutes. It was his misfortune that he happened to pass a police car parked in a lay-by. Observing this blatant contravening of traffic law, inevitably the officers followed in his wake, rapidly overhauling him.

They gave reason for stopping him, then demanded to know why he was driving in such a foolish and dangerous fashion. The answer was simple, honest and to the point; The right hand held his lunch, whilst the left was saluting a magpie. Fortunately for him this, on the surface, daft explanation was accepted; one of the officers was well aware of the superstition that when one saw a solitary magpie, that handsomely plumaged bird should be saluted, as not to do so would bring misfortune.

Now where this barmy custom came from, I know not, but it is widely observed – well, here in the Westcountry it certainly is. Quite recently, Ann and I had cause to rue this ritual as it almost wore us out. For magpies decided to nest in a tree at the bottom of our garden. Now when there were two present, it posed no problem but most of the time there was but one – thus the obligatory acknowledgement, with hand and arm, ensured by the time its progeny had hatched, grown and 'flown the nest', we were both in need of physiotherapy on our shoulders. At the time, each of us exhorted logic to come to the rescue and steer us away from this tiresome pursuit – but it did not and almost assuredly never will. Such is the grip exerted by superstition; one knows, deep down, it is generally total nonsense, yet rarely do we have the discipline to confront it.

I well remember another instance of irrational behaviour concerning a bird. Some years ago, as an insurance agent calling monthly on rural homes here in Devon, I did my regular call on an elderly lady (living deep in the countryside) to collect her monthly payment. Seeing me from her window as I was walking down the path, she opened the front door of her cottage, a £5 note in her hand.

She glanced down, then screamed, almost hysterically; 'A robin on the doorstep,' she cried. 'A death in the family.'

She hurtled back inside, slamming the door behind her, whilst the nosy but harmless robin flew away and I was left fiver-less. Why this delightful, most British of birds should be the harbinger of doom I do not know but this dramatic example of irrational, deeply rooted terror has stayed with me ever since.

The number of such idiocies are manifold and cover virtually every aspect of life, varying considerably on the scale of possible calamity which can result if not appeased. It is said to be unlucky if folk cross on the stairs – though for the one going up or coming down is not stated (perhaps for both); also, on a dining table, if knives are left crossed, family discord will ensue.

On a more positive note on the cutlery front, if a spoon is dropped, there could well be, in the short term, a baby born to the family. Such optimistic beliefs, however, are rare. Most of these 'old wives tales' forecast disaster rather than triumph. Ann and I, though not as terrorised by such dogma as some folk appear to be, do pay heed to many, indulging ourselves in the long held philosophy that it is unwise 'to tempt fate'.

Neither of us, however, has any fear regarding the number 13; we were both born on the thirteenth, though in different months.

Another illogicality for which we both have contempt is the failure of people, often of advanced years, to make wills. Often some of, generally, sound outlook follow this self-indulgent, selfish practice because they feel that if they do make wills it will hasten their deaths. Nonsense; it will in no way precipitate their demise, but will, when they eventually 'shuffle off' increase lawyer's bills to their families.

Dying intestate is an expensive business. Each to his own, though, as the saying goes; it is odd, however, that in an age dominated by the wizardry of technology and the influence of higher education, so very many of us still pay heed to illogical portents and beliefs.

28

Plymouth – the Cinderella City

*E*XCEPT for very brief periods working away from the area in my youth, I have spent my entire life in West Devon – the first 30 odd years on the Bere Peninsula, then 40 plus in Tavistock.

Thus they are places close to my heart and I feel privileged to have dwelt in them and hope to be spared to reside in the old 'stannary' town – birthplace of Sir Francis Drake – in tolerable health for a while yet. There is, however, somewhere close by which, though I've never been an inhabitant, has loomed large in my life and for which I have much affection – the characterful 'Ocean City' of Plymouth.

The reasons for this are manifold. Although not a Plymothian, much of my work, interests and leisure activities have been centred within this major, historical settlement over the almost eight decades of my life.

I worked there back in the 1960s, being a full-time fireman in the city brigade; for several years I was privileged to be a magistrate sitting in the court sited close to the Barbican; much of our shopping takes place there, whilst its cinemas and splendid Theatre Royal figure large when it comes to leisure activities and, not least, what little stoicism and strength of character that has come my way over the decades (not a lot, and assuredly not sufficient) is down to a virtual lifetime of following their infuriating, mercurial, baffling, much loved football team with the Scottish name.

Thus, this large, vibrant town on the banks of the Tamar, which laps the shores of the magnificent esplanade that is 'The Hoe', has been important in my life and I would suggest in the lives of vast numbers of people throughout Devon and Cornwall, not least in terms of employment; Devonport Dockyard – the biggest in Europe – has been, and remains, the largest private employer in the South West. Yet, despite this, the urban area comprising the three ancient towns of Devonport, Sutton and Stonehouse, with a population in excess of a quarter of a million, could be classed as the 'Cinderella city of Britain – short changed, ever underestimated and undervalued, never treated fairly, always denied access to 'the Ball'.

Sadly it has long been thus; the great Yorkshire born writer, J B Priestley, was guilty of ignoring the great Royal Navy port some 80 years back, for he published a book, greatly lauded as an accurate, perceptive and comprehensive guide to the regions, towns and cities of Britain. There is, however, a major flaw in this well crafted, erudite publication – in the author's eyes, England clearly ended at Bristol, the four South West counties being ignored, including the place from where the Pilgrim Fathers sailed, by far the largest conurbation in this extensive and significant English area.

In an age when communication in terms of both travel and contact were limited there might have been some small excuse for this but in this modern era, when Plymouth is ignored possibly even more, there can be none.

It afflicts so many aspects of our lives here in South Devon; shows and plays leave London, go on provincial tours and grace relatively small towns – but it is commonplace for the Ocean City, despite having one of the best theatres outside of the capital, to be missed out.

Well known department stores with branches in modestly sized boroughs often by-pass Plymouth, whilst many of those which are in the city do not stock items to be found in their shops elsewhere.

Governments are no better; for their investment in the South West in general, and in its most populous centre in particular, is lamentable – lower than in any other region of the land.

There is no motorway south of Exeter, and shamefully, Plymouth unacceptably – indeed, ludicrously – has no airport, when relatively small places such as Penzance and Newquay to the south have thriving ones. The investment for both public and private sectors has long been meagre compared to most of the British Isles. Largely due to this, although there is no major unemployment, wage levels are well below the national average – thus, so often, living standards likewise. Party politics would appear to play no part in this; for over the decades the nation has had governments of varying ideologies, whilst Plymouth and the wider region has elected MPs with radically different party loyalties, yet the relative disadvantage of the region and its main provincial municipality has never been addressed in adequate fashion.

It really is time that the 'Ugly Sisters' of indifference and neglect were ostracised, with at last the 'Cinderella' that is the 'three towns' of Plymouth being invited to 'the Ball', then courted by the 'handsome prince' of affluence and recognition.

29

Clubs & Societies

*I*T was, I believe, Groucho Marx, who stated he would never wish to be part of any club that would have himself as a member.

I don't know enough concerning this famous member of the Marx Brothers to make a judgment, but when assessing my own anti-social solitary nature, I could say likewise.

If I was welcomed into any grouping, then it would have to be with people of similar character – basically, miserable toads.

Fortunately for myself, and more importantly, for others, I have never had any desire to join anything, not even the Plymouth Argyle Supporters' Association, despite my immense admiration for this valiant, sorely tried band of brothers and sisters.

Mind you, it's possible I could be tempted – if actually it exists – to join the Diogenes Club of which Sherlock Holmes' brother, Mycroft, was a member; for this was a society for grumpy, reclusive men who, whilst they would gather to dine, drink and benefit from a relaxing ambience, rarely spoke to each other. As it is, I know of no such group and have no wish to join any other – this is just as well, as I have only once ever been invited to.

Having said all this, I do have respect and admiration for so many of the societies, clubs and associations which proliferate. Whilst most exist, naturally, for the pleasure and fulfilment of those within their ranks, so many also do much to improve the welfare and cohesion of their towns and communities.

The admirable Lions organise numerous events throughout the year creating fun and enjoyment for folk whilst at the same time raising considerable sums for charity.

The young men and women of Round Table do likewise, and their elders in Rotary and Inner Wheel do considerable good work for fellow citizens.

Also, of course, there is the magnificent Royal British Legion.

This exemplary organisation does so much – they have for the past 90-plus years – for the wellbeing of those and their families who have fought, and often died, for their country.

Then there are societies such as Probus, whose ranks are filled by retired businesspeople, social and working men's clubs (most open to females, also) plus amongst others, those dedicated to specific political parties.

However, these latter establishments often have members who are not enticed through the door in pursuit of ideology, but rather for such reasons as that their liquor prices are usually quite low and many will sport decent snooker tables.

There are societies devoted to specific interests; local history circles, gardening and flower arranging groups, music appreciation, reading groups – all such and more abound in towns and large villages. Their membership will generally be of both genders but there are several

So much for being invited to join the 'Ancient order of Buffaloes'.

organisations either dominated by, or reserved solely for, ladies. This fact is often illustrated, vividly, by their titles: the Townswomen's Guild, Mothers' Union, Young Wives and, best known of all, the admirable Women's Institute.

Despite the vast diversity of interests and pursuits available to women of all ages in this era, the WI retains sound membership numbers. Granted, some branches struggle to remain viable, but many find their numbers increasing. Possibly the reason for this is that whilst standards of decorum and manners are always maintained – zealously guarded – they seem not ever to live in the past. Though founded more than 120 years ago, they are very much of the modern world and contribute widely to the public good.

There are, too, societies either dominated by, or exclusively for men; most well known of these is one which has a worldwide membership – Free Masonry. There is, though, a paradox regarding this very long established outfit; for whilst there can be few, if any, global organisations whose existence is better known, because of the secrecy which shrouds it few beyond its membership know what it actually does.

My belief from what little I've heard is that the masons on the whole are a force for good. The covert nature of their proceedings, though, rightly or wrongly, does not endear them to folk in an age awash with news and instant information.

I wrote earlier that, on a solitary occasion, I was invited to join an association. Long ago I was asked if I wanted to be a member of the Ancient Order of Buffaloes. Though honoured – as well as surprised – at the invitation, politely I declined. I feared I might have to keep one in the house, feed it and take it for walks.

30

Spring Holiday

𝓕OR many years, Ann, her sister Margaret and myself have gone south on holiday in May.

A major plus is that no airports or ferry terminals are involved. All that is needed is a car, a modest amount of petrol and the meagre amount of stamina required to drive 60 miles. Thus, an hour and a half journey takes us over the Tamar to a glorious spot up the coast from Padstow.

Another plus is that often we will forsake a wet Tavistock and arrive at our rented cottage in sunshine – no great surprise, as the annual rainfall figures for this area of the Duchy are significantly lower than those for our home town, where climate is influenced by the mass of Dartmoor, not an expanse noted for drought.

This year our routine, on the whole, was not overly different, but there was a subtle change; the terraced cottage we have hired over the years was being renovated, so not available.

However, the one next door was, so we rented that instead. In theory there would be little difference between this dwelling and that which we knew well, but we were a touch over optimistic.

We were able to access the previous property simply by retrieving a key placed under a flagstone near the front door. Not the pinnacle of security, true, but straightforward.

The process for gaining entry here, however, was infinitely more complex; indeed, a bank vault would have been little harder to invade.

We had been given a code to punch in on a pad on the side of a small box clinging to the wall just outside the front entrance. Inside this container were keys.

Numbers were put in then lined up in accordance with instructions but nothing happened. The process was repeated, again without success. Stoically, my wife and sister-in-law, despite my blatant impatience and annoyance – tried a third time. Hallelujah! The lid of the box dropped down revealing the crucial keys. No problem regarding entry now – surely? Wrong.

The key was inserted into the lock, turned left then right; the door, which was of a size, weight and thickness that might well have repelled Genghis Khan and his fearsome Mongolian hordes, budged not a millimetre.

We tried again, and again, and yet again, tugging, pushing, thumping, swearing (well, I was).

Suddenly, it opened – perhaps the abuse I aimed was the reason for this. Whatever, we were inside.

Tea was made and a welcome snack devoured. The sun was beaming down so we planned to go out the back door onto the patio, overlooking the Camel Estuary. The theory was sound but again the execution nightmarish, for we were confronted with another barrier made, seemingly, with sufficient timber to construct a Viking longship.

We were about to abandon exhaustive efforts to open it,

feeling it would be easier to go upstairs and abseil down an outside wall, when at last it was ajar.

Ours not to reason why – rather, we hurtled out into the warmth. Our stay was brief as it started to rain.

Sadly, the day got much worse, for it was the final day of the league football season and Plymouth Argyle had to win to, almost certainly, avoid relegation. To probably the amazement of the Green Army, they did manage a victory and joy abounded – initially.

In the words of the old proverb, though, 'there's many a slip twixt cup and lip'; the Pilgrims' survival depended on fellow strugglers Southend United doing the decent – and widely expected – thing of failing to defeat the mighty Sunderland. However, the 'Shrimpers' made a mockery of the form book and won. Grim news indeed.

The imbibing of copious amounts of liquor did nothing to dull the pain; likewise the attempts of the two dear ladies with me to soothe: 'It's only a game,' said they. Only a game? 'You cannot be serious!'

Matters did improve, mind you, but despite decent weather it was not totally relaxing.

For one thing, there was a 'state of the art' television set which would probably pick up broadcasts from outer space, but the operating of which was beyond my comprehension. Thus I could only view when either Ann or Margaret were there to turn it on. Likewise there was a sophisticated microwave which fooled us all and a dishwasher which seemed selective as to what it actually cleaned. Despite all this though, Cornwall is a glorious part of the world, ever a joy to visit. To me, only 'Glorious Devon' can surpass it.

31

The Curse of Lids

WHEN it comes to food, I like strong, spicy flavours in savoury dishes and snacks, but paradoxically, overt sweetness in desserts and the like. With the latter, also often lashings of cream, especially of the clotted variety.

However, at midday we tend to go for the tangy – crusty bread, salty biscuits, Cambozola cheese for Ann, mature cheddar for me, perhaps a slice or two of smoked ham and so forth, all devoured with, in my case, liberal dollops of English mustard, chutney and pickled onions. Recently Ann and I had a morning slaving in the garden – well she did I made the excuse that we needed empty sacks so hurtled off to the local tip to dispose of the contents of half a dozen very full ones. The fact that the local recycling facility is often harder to break into than a bank vault meant, like Captain Oates, I was gone 'some time'.

Whatever, we sat down to a repast of the aforementioned piquant delicacies. Much to our taste though such victuals are, their flavour is intensified agreeably with the addition of the relishes listed earlier.

Now by coincidence all were new jars, so required

opening. The mustard was no problem but the two others were a daunting challenge.

First up were the onions. 'Herculean' has to be the word to describe our endeavours regarding removing the lid; whether King Kong had been employed to put it on I know not, but his services were definitely required concerning its removal.

Trying to unscrew it in ordinary fashion was beyond us, so we thumped the top and rim with the handle of a heavy knife, to no avail. A wet dish cloth was placed over the lid.

There followed a couple of minutes of wrestling with the beast, our hands and arms aching with the strain. Nothing. Did we surrender?

Assuredly not! Ann was born in the county which sent 'Cousin Jacks' to mine the world, whilst I'm a Devonian, thus born in the shire from which Drake and the famed 'Sea Dogs' sailed the oceans and saw off the Armada.

Undaunted, we tried fresh tactics, all of which involved huge effort and from my lips the occasional expletive – well, not that occasional.

With the notion coming to mind that metal expands when heated, a kettle was boiled with a part of its contents poured over the jar. A further crusade ensued, but sadly the onions remained unliberated.

The 'Dunkirk Spirit' did not desert us but we rationalised that, in reality, this epic event was not a victory but a retreat. Thus we withdrew from battle – the jar would be returned to the shop.

Attentions turned to the sealed pot of chutney; once more battle was joined. Several exhausting minutes followed, then the Eureka moment; through the sweat and tears which

f

coursed our faces we witnessed the dislodging of the barrier between ourselves and the tasty pickle. A tsunami of triumph engulfing us, we sat down to lunch. Fortunately, it not being a hot meal, delay did not affect its quality.

I piled ample provisions upon my plate, then added mustard. Accepting it would be pickled onion-less, I did not hold back on the chutney.

Seeing it drop from a spoon onto my plate, though, I became a touch apprehensive; it seemed rather runny and very red, so I tasted it. A very pleasant flavour indeed, but a more suitable additive to cream than cheese.

I looked at the label on the container – strawberry jam. I had taken the wrong pot from the larder! Ann, a most loyal, patient and forgiving lady, shook her head but refrained from comment. Suddenly, salvation – the kitchen door opened and we were joined by our grandson.

I switched the kettle on whilst Ann, registering rapidly the dramatic difference between the physique of this fine young man and that of her puny, gnarled husband requested he try to remove the recalcitrant pickle jar lid.

In seconds the contents were exposed to the air. Invited to tackle the chutney top, he took a touch longer (a thoughtful fellow, possibly deliberately to make it appear the initial challenge to us of opening the pickled onions – which we failed – was more formidable than it was in reality), but the contents were soon exposed.

Thus the lesson is clear; if these jars continue to be sealed so zealously, then every time we buy a new jar of relish, our supportive grandson will be invited to lunch.

Radio Comedy

32

$\mathcal{R}$EADING, a while back, of the death of that gifted comedy actress, June Whitfield, my mind was transported back to the radio comedy of my youth – the 1940s and 50s.

There might have been television humour as well, mind you, but seeing as my parents – like most of the nation – did not have a TV set until the late 50s, I would have no knowledge of such; and when we did acquire access to this revolutionary medium, what comedy there was appeared, predominantly, to be American – the likes of Jack Benny, Burns and Allen, I Love Lucy and, my favourite, Sergeant Bilko, starring the sparkling Phil Silvers.

The radio, though, that was a different matter; so many delightful programmes (well they were to me) proliferated.

Everything then was on the BBC; there was no independent or commercial radio, so it could be that the Government, conscious of the grim, dangerous times which were the war years, and the tough, austere era that was the decade following, encouraged a plethora of series designed to lift the spirits of the nation. Comedy, being probably the most vulnerable of all entertainment forms to individual taste, some broadcasts appealed to me far more than others; however, looking back, generally I enjoyed the wireless humour of those times infinitely more than that thrust at us nowadays which comes via sophisticated TV images beamed into our homes.

To be fair, this could be down, to an extent, to miserable me, for often I sit, poker faced, when gazing at the efforts of modern comics whilst those about me are convulsed with laughter. The lighthearted fare which, decades back, came into our homes via the long or medium waves was a different matter – I loved it (or most of it, at least). Which brings me back to the great June Whitfield. In a career that spanned some 70 years and more, and covered virtually everything – film, TV, radio, theatre – I remember her, initially, in a hugely popular wireless programme, Take It From Here. In this she played the female side of a gormless but hilarious couple, 'Ron and Eth'.

Australian comedian Dick Bentley was the obtuse Ron, whilst 'Professor' Jimmy Edwards fulfilled the role of 'Father'. During that era, also, came shows such as Ray's a Laugh, featuring the witty Ted Ray, plus the enormously popular, Hancock's Half Hour. Tony Hancock, clearly, was the star but he had a gifted supporting cast which included the popular Hattie Jacques and my favourite, the pugnacious Sid James, who went on to be a key member of the Carry On team.

A programme with a huge audience was Educating Archie, featuring Peter Brough and Archie Andrews. Many performers who went on to be 'big names' escaped anonymity thanks to regular slots in this weekly production, amongst them that gifted entertainer Max Bygraves, and, most notably, a lady who became a world superstar, Dame Julie Andrews.

Looking back, though, there was an almost ludicrous aspect to it all; for Archie was a wooden puppet, his voice provided by Mr Brough. As ventriloquism is surely a visual entertainment, to put it on a medium where lips cannot be seen was, in reality, daft. The 50s saw the arrival of a very different kind of humour – the anarchic Goons – Harry Secombe, Spike Milligan and Peter Sellers – all of whom went on to prominence. A completely new kind of comedy, folk tended to either love it or find it baffling. Sadly, my obtuse mindset put me into the latter camp. What did appeal, though, were a brace of creations of the early 60s – Beyond Our Ken and Round The Horne. In these shows, the urbane Kenneth Horne played the 'straight man', with a posse of gifted contributors, including the marvellous Kenneth Williams; magical.

Regretfully lack of space prevents me citing several other notable series which linger in the memory. Perhaps, though, I should pause for a moment of self analysis; I fear I might be a touch guilty of succumbing to that potential mischief maker, nostalgia.

These programmes were devoured in my childhood and youth when innocence reigned. Over 60 years later, if I listened to them again, it could be that cynicism and the 'slings and arrows' of a long life might well have swept away such naivety. Who knows and who cares – I enjoyed them at the time.

33

Cosset Your Car

*T*HE wellbeing of our car has long been important to us. We have never had a brand new one – indeed, in times past when 'pennies' were fewer, we drove some quite elderly machines the mileages of which registered as many digits as the cost of an average house these days.

No matter what its vintage, however, as we have ever lived in what is essentially a rural area, the possession of 'wheels' has been constantly, and remains, of importance.

Thus we have always tried to look after, possibly cosset, the sizeable number, and variety, of vehicles which have transported us over the decades.

Mind you, to tend to their mechanical needs has perpetually been beyond me. I can tell if it has enough petrol thanks to a gauge, whilst if low on water or oil, lights flash, but beyond this I am technically illiterate; put a spanner or screwdriver in my hands and I'm dangerous.

Being aware of such, I've always left rectification of problems to the professionals. Folk with the priceless ability to be able to cure the myriad ills which can afflict the internal combustion engine and other diverse maladies which can immobilise an automobile.

There is a direction, though, in which we've travelled consistently when it comes to protecting the motor upon which we rely so much – we ensure it is garaged at night (during the day, also, if not being used).

Thus on frosty mornings when many are making themselves late, plus wearing themselves out, using scrapers, or spraying expensive de-icers (or both) on windscreens, ours comes out of its snug kennel free from such impediment.

Also, generally – as the engine will not have become too cold or damp overnight – it will be tolerably easy to start. Rarely is one afflicted with the time consuming, stressful challenge of having, incessantly, to turn the engine over in the hope it stutters into life before the battery runs out.

A further plus in housing a car is the security aspect; it is vastly more difficult for a thief to purloin that which is under lock and key than an auto standing, forlornly, on the public road in front of a house.

Many, of course, dwell in properties which do not have garages or hardstandings; thus the public road is the sole home their personal transport can occupy; a number, though, do, but don't use them. There is a gent I know who recently had a newish BMW stolen from the street outside his home; the point here, though, is that it was not just left in front of his dwelling, it was standing a mere pavement's width from his garage.

When I enquired, politely but curiously, as to why it was not housed therein, he replied that the sizeable custom-built addition to his property was requisitioned for storage of bric-a-brac, furniture and the like which was aged and surplus to requirements.

Thus, parked vulnerably on a busy road, prey to the elements and any passing rogue (or vandal) was a quality limousine worth perhaps some £20,000, whilst locked securely in the garage was a conglomeration of junk much of which would disgrace a council 'tip'; and such is typical throughout the land – garages used as storerooms for trivia, valuable motors abandoned to their fate. I know of a fellow, a keen gardener who, as his greenhouse was demolished by a storm, now leaves his car on the road, using his double garage as a nursery and potting shed. Some motorists, in an effort to park their transport on their own property, create hardstandings; in principle, a sound idea but, once again, these are often not used for the intended purpose.

An acquaintance of mine had one created, but feeling the cement expanse was not pleasing to the eye, filled it with pot plants rather than her car.

A gent nearby also laid one, but being a builder by trade, stores his materials upon it, whilst I'm aware of someone else who not only installed a flagstoned base but also put a perspex roof over it. Does it house his 'wheels'? No – he and his spouse love barbecues; rapidly they found this covered, but outdoor area, ideal for alfresco cooking in our somewhat erratic weather.

To me all this defies logic – but it is their business; they break no laws. We, though, will remain dedicated car cosseters

34

Journey to Henley

ON a cloudy morning in June Ann and I headed north, making for Henley-on-Thames, not to view or participate in the world famous Royal Regatta – neither would have had allure for us – but rather to visit our son David and his partner, Rachel.

The journey towards Okehampton was pedestrian. We were stuck behind a heavily laden trailer pulled by a tractor of great age. Passing it at last, we made the dual carriageway. The traffic, while heavy, was moving at a tolerable pace. We got to the M5 which was very busy but still we managed to maintain some progress on our pilgrimage towards the South East, though it was laboured.

It became even more so just north of Exeter, where we were assaulted by rain of almost biblical proportions.

Being on a motorway it was virtually impossible to stop, so main beam on, windscreen wipers scurrying – and fervently praying – we proceeded.

After some ten minutes this holocaust of precipitation ceased. We had escaped unscathed, though a touch stressed, and gave a joint sigh of relief – surely all now would be well.

We were overly optimistic, for it was not long before we hit a stretch which possibly accommodated more cones than a pine forest.

There were flashing signs emblazoned with '50 mph' – if only! The tempo at which we proceeded for miles would not have taxed an arthritic tortoise, but while barriers, signs (some mentioning speed cameras), heavy plant and the like proliferated, actual workers were nowhere to be seen.

Still, eventually we escaped this long, tortuous chicane and were on the open road once more, my right foot thrusting the accelerator to the floor but only briefly. The approach to Bristol frequently is alien to traffic mobility, so it was on this 'Black Friday'; not roadworks, mind you, just an ocean of vehicles. Thus did we inch towards, then past, the mammoth Gordano service station.

Things did improve, however, and it was not too long before we approached the intersection of motorways.

Overhead signs and instructions abound, as do lanes – M4, West or East, South Wales or London, M5. North or South, plus a further major highway leading into Bristol. To choose the incorrect one would be calamitous, as an immense portion of both time and petrol could be consumed in attempting to escape. Ann's navigation was flawless and soon we were on the open highway heading east.

Sadly our swift forward movement was again short lived, for the torrent which had besieged us earlier in the journey returned – reinforced, it fell in proportions which suggested Noah could be back in business.

With visibility limited severely, we advanced at a rate so slow it would have shamed an elderly donkey. After some 20 minutes or more, the deluge ceased instantly and required momentum returned. As we thrust eastwards, we were very aware of an accident on the westbound carriageway causing a gargantuan tailback. We were sympathetic – and highly relieved it was not us.

The relevant exit reached at last, we escaped the motorway, heading towards Henley; our spirits rose. However, a mile from the famous old town we halted. A static tailback of vehicles. Bound to move soon, surely?

It did not. After a while, some cars in the line turned about, then made for a narrow lane on the opposite side of the road. Ann felt we should ignore their example; she is though, married to one of the world's most impatient men. Figuring these drivers were local thus knew the terrain, I heeded not her advice – and followed them.

Several miles of narrow, winding lanes ensued. Eventually turning a severe corner, we saw Henley to our right. Directly in front though, we were confronted with another log jam of motors. Once more folk started doing three point turns – well, more like seven point in such a narrow road. Instantly, and stupidly, I decided to do likewise – and promptly reversed into a granite post. Ann insisted we remained where we were. Defeated. I turned off the engine.

After some 20 minutes, traffic started to move – crucially we were soon crossing the only bridge over the Thames leading into the town which, for well over an hour, had been blocked by a broken down lorry – hence the gridlock.

Greeting our lovely family at last after a 6 hour-plus journey felt like discovering the Holy Grail. Their hospitality for the weekend was surpassed only by the pleasure of their company. We will return, of course, but next time it could be far less traumatic if we hire a small plane, then parachute down onto their lawn!

35

Amazing Theatre

WATCHING sport can be enjoyable, entertaining, absorbing, traumatic; if one follows Plymouth Argyle it can also threaten one's health.

There are occasions though – albeit, rare – when sporting duels, based as they are on human conflict (generally of a civilised nature) can rise above levels of determined, even inspired endeavour, and become riveting theatre. Such will be exceptional instances when an event looms large in the national consciousness, when much is either expected or hoped for, when stakes are at their highest, and which, subsequently, produce excellence of a truly mesmeric nature – a brilliance which can inspire all privileged to witness it. These times are scarce, but when they occur they linger long in the memory. The first time I recall such was well over 60 years ago – a Saturday afternoon in May 1953. Along with seemingly half the population of Bere Alston, I was squashed into the front room of one of the few folk on the peninsula who possessed a television set. It was the first time I had ever seen TV; mind you, one had to have excellent eyesight to see anything, the screen little bigger than the cover of the average novel. A football match flickered before us – the FA Cup Final, an all Lancashire affair.

Inhabitants of the town of Bolton naturally wanted their Wanderers to win; the bulk of the nation, though, were rooting for opponents Blackpool. The reason? Simply because wearing the colours of the Seasiders was the nation's most venerated sportsman, the iconic Stanley Matthews. Virtually all the honours which football, world wide, could bestow had come the way of the 'Wizard of Dribble'; however, a notable exception was an FA Cup winner's medal. He being almost 40, this was viewed as his last opportunity. With just over 20 minutes of the match remaining it seemed the prize would again elude him. Wanderers were winning, deservedly, by three goals to one. Suddenly, as if his shoulder had been touched by the hand of God, the great winger turned on his magic. He laid on a goal for Stan Mortensen, then a second and, in the last minute, the winner by Bill Perry. Poor Bolton were devastated, but the nation rejoiced. Stanley had his trophy at last. This is still classed as the greatest ever cup final – assuredly it was absorbing drama, theatre never to be forgotten.

A year later we witnessed Roger Bannister, his face contorted with effort, and probably pain, galloping around a cinder track in Oxford in the process of running the first ever sub four minute mile; as he almost fell, exhausted, over the finish line, we knew we had the privilege of witnessing sporting history.

A lifelong boxing fan, I was witness in the early 1960s to that, which to me, was possibly the most sensational and dramatic moment in the annals of British pugilism in my lifetime. That esteemed and exceedingly popular British Heavyweight Champion, Henry Cooper, fought the highly charismatic 'Louisville Lip' at Wembley before a vast crowd. Cassius Clay was the man's real name, though he was to convert to Islam, calling himself Muhammed Ali, now a sporting legend. A few months later he was to become world champion, defeating the fearsome Sonny Liston. The rest, as the saying goes, is history. Certainly he was expected to beat 'Our Henry' with ease, and this he was doing; then, in the fifth round, Cooper, who had the hardest punch in world boxing, caught him with a left hook – his famed 'hammer'. Clay hit the canvas, clearly out; it was late in the round, though, and he was 'saved by the bell'. Then – infamy. His trainer, seeing he needed time to recover, cynically slashed one of his gloves. By the time a new one was fetched and fitted, Clay had recovered enough to go on to win. The instant, though, when this sublimely gifted fighter was laid horizontal was pulsating drama.

As indeed was England winning the football World Cup in 1966; the score all square at the end of normal time, the land of Saint George clinched it, gloriously, in the final minute of the extra half hour. This moment, as Geoff Hurst's shot was hurtling towards the back of the net, was summed up for posterity by TV commentator Kenneth Wolstenholme, with those oft quoted words, 'some people are on the pitch, they think it's all over; it is now.'

Likewise the Rugby World Cup in 2003, when that sublime fly-half Jonny Wilkinson saw off the Aussies on their own turf, again 'at the death', with a brilliant drop goal.

Also how about England's recent victory versus New Zealand in the Cricket World Cup – arguably the most exciting, dramatic encounter in the long history of the game? Awesome and unforgettable.

Mind you, regularly do the 'Green Army' witness theatre at Home Park. Sadly, however, it is likely to be tragedy – though one does occasionally confront farce.

36

Baths & Showers

WHEN it comes to personal ablutions, I have always
preferred baths to showers.

The Romans, with their genius for efficient plumbing,
were largely responsible for creating the first; the second,
until reasonably modern times, was left to meteorology to
bestow – or perhaps it is the Lord (or Lady) who is in
charge; if so, he or she has a habit of sending them
randomly and in radically varying quantities.

Certainly, few houses would have contained showers
back in my youth. Indeed, the only ones I can recall were
at school. One would come into the dressing room caked
with mud after playing football or rugby, to be assaulted –
and only partially cleansed – by a volley of cold water,
though it was not supposed to be of such a low
temperature. The explanation for this rigorous, often
freezing, attack was that either the thermostat had
malfunctioned, or that there was a defect in the mechanism
which was meant to heat it in the first place. Whatever, it
was not a joyful experience.

In my view, a bath has ever been more reliable and

pleasurable. In fact, I've perpetually looked upon taking a shower as being a basic means of maintaining cleanliness, whereas a bath has always been a source of pleasure and relaxation.

Mind you, until the age of 11, all my soaks – that of all our family – took place in a long tin receptacle which would be placed in front of the ancient range in our farm kitchen, filled from kettles and saucepans heated on the hot plates.

Temperature control was down to my mother's judgement, done literally by hand. After this, my parents made a massive forwards step towards the modern age – a bathroom was installed, plus an indoor toilet. No more fraught, freezing forays, especially at night, to the archaic outdoor facility.

Following this, except for a rare stay in a hotel or guesthouse, rarely did I encounter showers, and if I did they were my second choice if there was the option of a bath. In our house now, we have both, but in this modern age, numerous dwellings possess that system which drenches rather than soothes.

Space, of course, is part of the reason for this as a high percentage of homes these days, in pursuit of maximising bedroom numbers, have bathrooms seemingly little larger than rabbit hutches, thus insufficient space for even the smallest bath. Indeed, often the shower cubicle will struggle to house anybody of above average proportions.

As to the mechanism itself, one tends to wonder if any manufacturer created more than one of any given model. For virtually every house appears to have something different installed. If lucky, one can stand under the nozzle, simply push a button, and be doused with a comforting spray of pleasingly warm water. So many, though, possess mechanisms which are way beyond a technophobe such as myself. In fact, one feels that a few can only be activated if one contacts mission control.

It's very different with baths, however. There are two taps, one sporting hot water, the other cold – even an idiot like me can master its operation. As to the warmth of the water required for a relaxing sojourn, assessment is simple. A hand thrust beneath the surface will suffice and the depth is a matter of personal choice.

One of our sons has gallonage which I would never seek to emulate as I am unable to swim, but I do like to luxuriate, at considerable length, in an enamelled receptacle in which one can lay out fully.

Being such an advocate when it comes to personal cleanliness of the horizontal over the vertical, the puzzle to me is as to why so many, clearly the majority, take an opposite view. Could it be the age in which we live, for it is an era when folk's lives appear to be hectic, one in which the poet's lament that 'we have no time to stand and stare,' becomes ever more apparent and, to me, sad.

Many will see a session on a computer, a viewing of Facebook or Twitter, a series of text messages to friends and family, plus numerous other distractions and perceived priorities which did not exist a generation ago, as being a vastly more satisfying, indeed vital, use of their time than lying for a goodly period in a bath. So be it. As the saying goes, 'each to their own'. As for myself, a creature of habit, and someone who likes his comfort, whilst busy weekdays demand the efficient brevity of showers, weekends will remain devoted to the self indulgence of baths.

37

The Trauma of No Signal

*B*ACK in July – from New York – came to stay two of our granddaughters; their mother, father and brother were to follow.

My input towards their welfare and entertainment was minimal, their grandmother, Ann, fulfilling the role with aplomb. My only positive contribution was to act as chauffeur when we took them around our glorious West Country – blessed, fortunately, with fine weather.

Used to the urban sprawl that is Manhattan, they found climbing rocks at Merrivale exhilarating fun, while local beaches had far more allure than Coney Island. An extended session on a zipwire in a first class, but under used, play park in Bere Ferrers was chosen in preference to a visit to the cinema; truly outdoor girls. Food wise, pasties were chosen for lunch rather than burgers, so at heart they are Devon 'maids' despite living so far away.

So went well the week. With them due to go up to London to their other grandparents on the Saturday, at breakfast on the Friday, Ann and I mused as to what should be the itinerary that sunny morning. We were interrupted dramatically; there was a wailing from upstairs, then a clattering of feet descending, and we were confronted by the elder of the girls.

Though only 13, she is quite mature, yet clearly was distraught. What could be wrong?

News of Plymouth Argyle's relegation had engulfed us months before so it couldn't be that; the name of the new Prime Minister had still to be revealed so that wasn't the cause of such angst, whilst there had been no very recent twists to the saga that is Brexit – and she was too young for it to be an affair of the heart.

Concerned grandparents, we jumped up from the table to console her and to ascertain that which ailed her.

The latter was infinitely easier than the former. 'It's my phone,' cried she, her face almost ashen, 'it won't work. I've tried everything but it's dead. I don't know what to do.'

There are some problems in life with which I can give help, but being the chronic technophobe that I am, assuredly this was not amongst them. Ann is light years beyond me in such knowledge, yet her awareness is limited. Whatever, she asked the basic questions – had it been charged, had she encountered problems recently and the like.

The traumatised young lady could think of no reason why this small but sophisticated appliance, crucial in her life, refused to operate.

Clearly, to her, this was a calamity of mega proportions. Something had to be done, though her initial suggestion was not thought through.

For she wished to seek advice from her parents, but as they were on the other side of the Atlantic, it was doubtful they could be of much help; a rare moment of inspiration on my part, I pointed out it would be the middle of the night in New York. Mind you, rapidly was I relegated back to idiot status when I opined that the device be given a solid thump (it had sometimes been effective with televisions).

Ann suggested charging the battery again, whilst I, a touch more logical than normal, pointed out it might need replacing; it went back on charge. We would give it an hour – if then there was no joy, urgent action would be essential if a nervous breakdown was to be avoided. Never did 60 minutes pass so slowly, especially for our granddaughter. At the end ot it, she snatched the phone from the charger – and tried it. Nothing. Totally dead.

Not only was she becoming ever more stressed but the whiteness of her texting digit suggested it was suffering from lack of circulation; gangrene could well set in.

Ann advised we go down immediately to the town to seek the help of those working in the mobile phone shop. Instantly granddaughter and I were up the path and away; my plan was to drop the distressed young lady at the crucial venue, then go to the church to pray.

There was no need; for the young fellow in the store, hearing of the problem gazed at it for just a few seconds, then appeared to merely stroke it. Within seconds it was working, our granddaughter was exhilarated – I was massively relieved – and, gentleman that he was, he charged not a penny.

A quick thump used to work with televisions!

38

Names & Pseudonyms

*T*O me, the idiosyncrasies of human nature never fail to fascinate, indeed, at times bemuse – being a rather obtuse soul, the latter especially.

Not least amongst that which I find odd with many folk is the desire to change their names – sometimes just the one, often both.

Now if someone has something to hide or are seeking a fresh start in life, then it can make sense; but that which puzzles is why a number who seek success, and achieve it, do so under titles which were not theirs at birth.

Personally, as all the failures of my life have been in the names with which I was baptised, if ever I was able to achieve eminence (highly unlikely) then assuredly I would want to enjoy it under that name also – not modest, true, but surely satisfying.

Numerous famous men and women, though, have gained renown in 'monikers' which they themselves have created. In the film and show business world they abound and always have.

Mind you, there are occasions one can see why there

possibly was a need for one's real sobriquet to be abandoned. A major example of such was John Wayne, whose real name was Marion Morrison; one would have to concede that it would have been a touch hard to take seriously a 'Marion' who spent most of his career hurtling across cinema screens chasing desperados.

Then there is Michael Caine – born Maurice Mickelwhite; nothing wrong with that, of course, but it would never roll smoothly off the tongue. However, when he received his knighthood it was in accordance with the label given him by his parents; thus it's clear he is proud of it, and only changed it in furtherance of his career.

Archie Leach, born in Bristol, became Cary Grant, whilst that Hollywood legend of the 1930s, the Swedish Greta Garbo, was, in reality, Greta Lovisa Gustafsson; here one can fully see the need for change – there's no way the 'Yanks' would have got to grips with that.

That heart-throb of the twenties, Rudolph Valentino, was given names contained 47 letters; however, it's hard to understand why a gent whose title comprised a mere nine digits – Reg Dwight – decided to become Elton John; mind you, it clearly worked.

Now whilst it's possible to appreciate why some in the entertainment world feel their prospects are enhanced by amending what they were called originally, there are other spheres in which it happens that almost baffle; the literary field is one such.

Why does anyone with the skills and erudition to be a successful writer wish to do so under a pseudonym? Heaven knows – yet many have done so, and do so, a number famed and honoured.

145

g

The name 'Samuel Langhorne Clemens' – resonates, yet he changed it to Mark Twain – the words of measurement of two fathoms he would hear called out when he was a ship's pilot on the Mississippi; would his deserved fame have been diminished had he retained his given title? Surely not; and there is that perceptive short story teller, O Henry (the 'O' is just a letter, an affectation); he was christened, William Sidney Porter – why change that?

It was somewhat different with nineteenth century 'man of letters' Sir Arthur Quiller-Couch; he did not change his name – rather he decimated it, writing under the single letter, 'Q', whilst that masterly wordsmith George Orwell (Eric Blair) apparently took his pen-name out of consideration for his parents. His promulgation of Socialism would, he feared, embarrass them, so he titled himself after a Lancashire river.

Mind you, it is not only the honoured and treasured who amend their 'handles' – two of the great 'monsters' of history did likewise.

Adolf Hitler's original surname was Schicklgruber; one feels the mesmeric effect he seemed to have over the German race could have been diluted a little had he stuck with it.

Then there was Joseph Stalin; he was christened – wait for it – Iosif Vissarionovich Dzhugashvili. Soviet journalists of the time must have been relieved he took a six letter epithet where there was little scope for error; spelling correctly his real name, though, would have been a nightmare, getting it wrong an even greater one – either a spell in a Gulag, or worse, a confrontation with a firing squad.

Generally speaking, though, I see little purpose in the amending of that which one is called – though there are exceptions; for if I was burdened by the 'labels' which some parents give their children, often in acts of gross self-indulgence, I would change them the very day I reached manhood.

39

Dance

*T*HERE are few things in life which give me greater pleasure than to watch dance, in virtually all its forms, which are manifold; ballet, tap, flamenco, folk, morris, country, jive, Latin American, ball-room (though 'Strictly' is rarely viewed as it has been hi-jacked by hype and yap, with the dancing almost an afterthought).

Most dancing though, I enjoy viewing whether it be live, on television or on film. There is an irony in this, however, for I cannot – and never have been able – to dance a single step; it is one of the minor tragedies of my life.

In this instance, it is not down to lack of effort or desire; no, it has ever been due to a failure in communication between my brain and my feet. My brothers were excellent dancers; indeed, my sibling Stan, as a youth, folk danced in the Albert Hall. Also, in my younger days, most of my peers seemed, at least, proficient, when it came to the popular movements of the day – waltzes, quick-steps, jive and the like; I, however, was limited to the 'hokey cokey', which could probably have been mastered by a duck billed platypus. In my defence, I did decide to do something about it – I went to dancing classes. To say I was a failure would be a massive understatement; I was as inept after a dozen sessions as I had been at the start. The teacher, clearly feeling a touch guilty at taking my money yet failing to 'deliver', suggested I abandon my attempts to emulate Astaire. Knowing she was right, I did so and have been condemned to a lifetime of isolation from the dance floor.

Sadly this has meant that Ann has largely been denied 'tripping the light fantastic' – which, though she doesn't mention it, has to disappoint her. For she is an excellent dancer, able to glide across the floor to Johann Strauss, jive to Buddy Holly; also, she can put in a vibrant performance at a Scottish ceilidh; she has taken to the floor with friends over the decades, but not often. On occasions, when my inhibitions have been partially neutralised by liberal portions of wine, I have joined her; the dance has to be exceedingly slow, mind you, requiring little movement of legs and feet. Indeed, a bookend would probably achieve more mobility. In recent years she has done some line dancing; this has the merit of not needing a partner.

Now, when I consider my ineptitude regarding the art of graceful movement, it puzzles me somewhat that I do so enjoy watching it in others. Mind you, I am, in my tastes – as in most arenas – traditional and conservative; little modern dance appeals. This certainly is true of ballet; 'Swan Lake', 'La Fille Mal Gardée', and the like, always delight – often the music almost as much as the choreography. The present day, though, whilst I can appreciate the grace of performers, has little allure. Shows such as 'The Blue Danube' and 'Merry Widow' with their glorious waltz music, colour and panache are truly a joy, whilst so many postwar Hollywood musicals have spellbinding sequences; Gene Kelly getting drenched in 'Singing in the Rain', that awesome sequence in 'Seven Brides for Seven Brothers' when a wooden barn is built to pulsating music by the brothers – magnificent in terms of both creativity and performance. Then there is the magical, mind-blowing, riveting sequence from 'West Side Story' – danced and sung on a rooftop by the Puerto Ricans to the joyously frenetic rhythms and words of Leonard Bernstein's 'America'.

Supreme to me, though, was the fellow mentioned a little earlier – Fred Astaire. On occasions those old 'black and white' musicals of the 1930s come on television, and always I watch them. The storylines are often plain daft, but such are of little importance; for they feature the great Fred, brilliantly supported by a sublime partner in Ginger Rogers, gliding across the floor, his feet, at times, little more than a blur; and often, when performing solo, he would elevate tap dancing to a level surely never surpassed, his shoes thudding the stage with the mesmeric insistence of a 'tom tom'. To think that when early in his career, he auditioned for a small part in a film, the director stated in his assessment of this subsequent legend, 'can't act, can't sing, can dance a little'.

In reality he could do all three – the last, divinely. Clearly there can be no sense of failure in not being able to dance like him, but I will always regret that I've never been able to master the art to just the modest level which would have enabled me to dance with my lovely Ann.

40

The British Have Weather

*I*T has been said that whereas other countries have 'climate', the British have weather; assuredly we have had copious amounts of it this past year. Hot, at times searing, sunshine abounded during the summer, but, then again, so did lashing, torrential rain (often causing flooding), whilst there were, on occasions, gales whose wind velocity would not be surpassed during winter. Virtually all this, it is claimed, is down to that destructive and civilisation threatening enemy known as either 'global warming' or 'climate change' (personally I believe the latter to be a better description).

Now, possessing the scientific knowledge of a backward mule, I would not presume to argue with eminent meteorologists who claim there is irrefutable evidence the world is on an upwards curve, temperature wise, and that the future threatens more extreme conditions than we have known in the past. What I do take issue with, however, is the oft stated 'recollections' of folk of more mature years that in their youth seasons were infinitely more reliable; often they recall autumns as being gentle and balmy, with sometimes an 'Indian Summer', whilst winters in their memory were frosty with a little snow, but there would usually be sufficient rainfall to fill the reservoirs. Spring would bring pleasant sunshine which, allied to April showers, made the flowers and grass grow.

As to summer, this was a glorious time when sunshine dominated, life could be lived outdoors and, like Camelot, life giving rain fell only at night.

So many people I know of a similar vintage to myself tend to think of it like this, especially the school holidays in July and August, when, to their mind, never a raindrop fell during daylight hours; thus an idyllic outdoor lifestyle could be pursued for six weeks and more. I remember it differently, however – and I would possibly claim, respectfully, that due to personal experiences and background, my recollections could be a touch more accurate. For I am the son of farmers and market gardeners whose livelihood depended, in large measure, on weather, and I can still recall, quite vividly, the bounty which accrued when the elements were benevolent and the calamities which would afflict when they were not. Often hay and corn harvests were gathered easily and rewardingly in warm, dry conditions; some years, though, much would not be harvested at all, at times seemingly incessant precipitation making it hard to impossible, to gather the crop.

If there was a heatwave, that vital cash crop, strawberries, would at times ripen faster than they could be picked, whilst in other years if conditions were excessively wet, the fruit would rot on the plants; both calamitous in financial terms. Potatoes, likewise, would perish in the ground when the 'rain gods' ran rampant. Clearly there were some delightful summers – and school vacations – but far fewer than many remember. There were also droughts brought about by abnormal heat and, of course, a serious lack of rainfall. 1959 was such an annum and, famously, 1976 when there was scarcely any moisture falling from the sky for about five months; blistering heat, though, was almost a daily occurrence. Not only farmers suffered here, for chronic water shortages brought about closure of factories and there was severe water rationing for millions throughout the land, leading to standpipes in the streets.

Winters, too, were unreliable in terms of rainfall, frosts and the like. Again my farming memories loom large; often the land would be saturated, buildings and trees bludgeoned by gales – fields reduced, rapidly, to a sea of mud. Thus farm animals had to be fed precious hay and other fodder, grass submerged in the morass; also it was detrimental to them in health terms – sheep especially are weakened in such conditions, they being equipped to resist the cold, rather than the wet. Then, now and again, there were 'Arctic' interludes; January and February of 1947 were such months – though being very young, I can only just remember it; far more vivid in my consciousness are the first three months of 1963 which produced probably the longest unbroken spell of severe winter conditions of the twentieth century.

Mind you, there were periods in the 18th and 19th centuries when severe winters were endured; indeed it was not unusual for the Thames to freeze over. There is, though, a 'flip side to the coin', in that the 12th century saw French wine growers complain their sales were being undermined by cheap imports from England – clear evidence that, overall, temperatures then were greater than they are today.

Now, despite what I've written, I do not suggest our weather patterns are not changing; I believe they probably are. However, surely it is important to be aware that these great islands of ours have always endured 'weather' and it seems most likely that this will continue.

41

The Flu Jab

*T*HE voice on the phone was terrifying a piercing, staccato tone which was akin to what, one surmises, a female Dalek's would be.

To be fair, it did not shriek 'exterminate' – rather the opposite. Although delivered in a timbre of such intensity it could be warning of an imminent nuclear attack, the contents of the call were positive; 'this is a message for Edward Harold Sherrell,' it rasped, then proceeded to state that due to age I am eligible for an anti-flu jab, so must contact my GP immediately.

The demanding instruction ended as abruptly as it had started. I put down the receiver; although grateful the NHS were sufficiently concerned for my welfare they were prepared to give me free preventative medication, at that moment I felt I needed something to soothe frayed nerves – perhaps even to avoid a heart attack.

I was beginning to get back to normal when once more the phone trilled; I answered it and, again, was assaulted by the 'Dalek'; it was a similar tirade, but this time directed at Ann. Replacing the receiver, I sought much needed fortification; unfortunately it cannot be got on prescription but the contents of a bottle marked 'single malt' can work wonders.

The 'amber nectar' having had a calming effect on me, both Ann and I felt it was wise to 'grasp the nettle' and contact the surgery to arrange appointments before they ran out of serum – as had happened the previous year.

The ringing at the far end went on for some time before a voice cut in; again, though, it did not sound remotely human. Granted, it didn't have the chilling, doom laden intonation of the earlier calls but it was spoken in an accent which offended this pedantic, but patriotic old toad.

Now the information given was that no human operative was available to speak to me 'all our stations are currently occupied; please call later.' This was annoying enough but which also grated was that the words were spoken in an American sounding accent; and stations'? I thought those were where one went to catch a train or bus.

I did try later – but the 'Yank' answered once more. Summoning the spirit which made the nation great, I determined not to be beaten – I left it a couple of hours, then had a further go. This time it was answered promptly, the voice definitely human, and British; it was, though, recorded – 'this surgery is now closed'; it went on to suggest I phone the following morning, although if it was an emergency a helpline number was given. Arranging flu jabs could not, in fairness, be classed as such, but even if it was I doubt we would have used it; for I did once in the past, and after being put through to a plethora of different departments and getting nowhere at a debilitating rate, I gave up.

'According to our records it's time to –
Vaccinate!'

Still, we being of an age when it is wise to take advantage of aids designed to maintain reasonable health I determined to make contact the following day. My spirits rose – quite promptly it was answered; a human being, at last? No – it was the American lady still informing that all 'stations' remained inundated. Utterly frustrated, a six letter word beginning with B and ending with R flew from my lips; I decided I would not bother with the medical profession but, rather, would dose myself with sufficient 'nectar' to neutralise (possibly) the unpleasant, potentially dangerous illness that is influenza. Ann, though, pointed out wisely, it would pay us both to confront the needle and suggested I visit the practice the next day and make appointments in person. Though not that keen, I had to concede that it would be far cheaper than dosing myself with Scotch.

Thus the following morning found me in a long queue shuffling forward, very slowly, towards the two ladies on reception at the far end of the spacious waiting area; customers' abounded – we do not seem to be a nation in the best of health. At last I was next on; I stated my business, saying an appointment, any time on any weekday would be fine. The lady was courteous but negative; 'we only do them on a Saturday – and the upcoming one is fully booked; but I can fit you in at the end of next month.'

Defeated, I nodded acquiesence, received printed details, thanked her and went home. Fortunately the lurgy had not seized us prior to our jabs – and they'd not run dry of serum. However, I'm not sure I will bother next year – though I could well be intimidated by that petrifying 'Dalek'.

42

Cars, Comfort & the Law

A WHILE back I had to take our car to the garage as the interior heating was working well below capacity. Having the blood of a lizard thus probably able to feel cold in a sauna (though I'm not certain on this as I've never been in one), wherever I am, including in a motor, I desire heat levels the like of which would grow cannabis.

So whilst the under performing warming system was not calamitous as it did not affect the mobility of the vehicle, to me it was a fault which needed rectifying immediately; thanks to the diligent efforts of the gent who nurses our machine, it was.

Whilst driving from the repair centre, however, I did feel 'wimpish'. For here I was making something of a drama despite the fact the car had been, to any normal mortal, tolerably warm even before the heating had been fully restored, when in my younger days few cars had any means at all of creating internal warmth.

Back then, when travelling in freezing weather, extra layers of clothes were added. It set me thinking as to just how different – even primitive – were the automobiles of those times compared with now.

There was no power steering; thus a driver did not so much guide a steering wheel as wrestle with it; the reality that vehicles, usually, were heavier then than nowadays made piloting them hard work.

There were no automated windows and often no mechanical means of indicating a change of direction; thus all signals to other road users were via a hand signal thrown out an open window.

No radios were to be found, often no internal lights, no windscreen washers or means of demisting windows; regularly water levels in the cooling reservoir needed checking, likewise oil in the sump, as engines consumed far more of both than they do today; petrol also – the less sophisticated mechanisms of those days propelling a car fewer miles per gallon than modern counterparts. Mind you, those times had their pluses; for whilst comfort, reliability and performance of autos were inferior, the laws which regulated the road user were infinitely laxer, and many which now control the actions and behaviour of motorists – often rigorously enforced – did not exist at all.

Speed cameras were yet to be invented, so although one could, theoretically, be 'done' for speeding, usually only an excessive pace would attract the attention of the police; and there were no breathalysers – a motorist would have to be virtually paralytic to be charged with drink driving.

Few rules governed the occupancy of conveyances, the requirement for the fitting and using of seat belts coming decades later. Thus, often, cars carried as many passengers – including children – as would fit in; and the state of motors was of scant interest to the authorities; thus 'old bangers' proliferated. I drove one myself (though I must confess, to my shame, it was not so when I bought it). Things changed (in theory at least) in the mid sixties when all vehicles over a certain age had, like today, to obtain an MOT certificate.

Mind you, those early inspections, in my experience, bore no resemblance to the stringent, often stressful examinations now. Obtaining my first MOT pass was, in fact, simplicity itself – and cheap. I drove my jalopy onto the forecourt of my local garage one winter's morning expecting to have to leave it for the day; I was wrong – the entire process was both speedy and painless.

Entering the snug office, I sat down opposite the owner. Seemingly seeing these new rules as a means of making a few easy 'bob', rapidly he laid the appropriate form on the desk before him; he glanced out the window at my decrepit Hillman Minx then asked questions. 'Brakes all right?' followed by like enquiries as to the state of the lights and steering, to which I exaggerated by replying, 'Yes'. 'How about the tyres?' Seeing as all were as smooth as Kojak's pate I had, in conscience, to admit they were a 'touch' worn. Clearly my reply was ignored for I was issued with a certificate which gave my wreck a clean bill of health for the next year.

I was out of the office and on my way before he changed his mind and decided to actually inspect it. Still, poetic justice was done a few weeks later; the chassis, rusted, collapsed; the Hillman was done for and a scrap dealer lowered his standards by towing it away. This was, of course, a very different age; standards now, quite rightly, are vastly more stringent. Vital on present day cluttered highways; a major minus, though – MOTs now cost hugely more than a few bob.

43

You Can't Go Wrong

*I*T was an invitation we simply could not refuse, friends of Ann and myself inviting us for a cream tea at the new house they had just purchased in the Tamar Valley.

Instructions were given as to how to find and access it so, as in theory, I know the area quite well, I had no doubt the venue, less than a dozen miles from our home, would be located with relative ease – and if there were to be any problems, I have the good fortune to be married to a lady of astute navigational skills. Having said this, though, at the end of the phone call issuing the invite, our prospective host threw in that chilling phrase, regarding the location of their new home, 'you can't go wrong' – possibly doom laden words when one considers they were directed at a man who might well walk past Buckingham Palace and not notice it.

Whatever, on the day of our promised mid-afternoon westcountry feast, we set off to see our friends; the journey, logically, should have taken less than half an hour; sadly logic did not feature prominently. No problem to start with, mind you – roads and lanes I've travelled over many a long year were covered at a leisurely, but unbroken pace. Then, turning a bend in a narrowish highway, our progress was halted – the road ahead, the one we needed to take, was shrouded in bollards, in front of which was a large yellow sign with a black arrow upon it pointing right, plus the word, 'Diversion'; we took it. Though mildly annoying, it caused no major problems as I was confident the lane we were on – so narrow the foliage upon the Devon hedge was touching both sides of the car – would take us, roughly speaking, in the correct direction for our destination. Soon, though, we confronted a problem – a herd of cows, brown in hue.

What they were doing there, we knew not; probably a gate somewhere had been left open, and the bovines had decided to seek pastures – if only hedgerows, new. There appeared to be no human presence. What to do? Retreat, sadly, was the sole option; the milkers, possibly 30 or 40 of them, were the most solid of barriers. Thus I had to reverse back towards the beginning of the lane, roughly a mile away. Such a manoeuvre would never have been easy, but now the stiffness and rather blurred judgment of old age made progress (if headway there was) exceedingly laboured. Eventually we got back to the diversion sign, turned about, and headed back the way we had come.

Suddenly I espied a narrow lane leading off to the left. Now whilst it had been several years since I had last negotiated these byways, I seemed to recall that this track, inauspicious though it appeared, would lead us to within half a mile of the hamlet we were seeking. Ann was not convinced, pointing out there being sufficient grass sprouting in the centre of it to sustain the herd from which we had just escaped; thus, she argued, it must lead somewhere very remote, as it was so little used. I, however, was convinced this thoroughfare, humble though it was, would deliver us close to where we wished to be – thus did I turn into it.

Slender and winding, the trail tapered even more with no decrease in its twists. After what seemed several miles we emerged into a road which, though still modest in width, was in comparison, like the M5. I stopped and looked around; it was not reassuring – I did not know where we were, but was brutally certain we were not where I thought we would be. Ann looked at me despairingly but kindly refrained from comment. What to do? With not a signpost in sight, mild panic began to take hold; then though – salvation.

Around a corner came a vast tractor pulling a trailer; I jumped from the car, waved it down, and explained to the farmer our predicament. The gent gave me a withering look, but refrained from comment except to point out we were about five miles from our destination – and heading in the opposite direction. Ann, having joined us, noted, mentally, the directions he gave us – crucially important, as the only instruction I could remember was that we had to turn around.

The farmer's directions were accurate and my wife's navigation impeccable; thus did we arrive at the hamlet we were seeking.

'What's the name of the house?' Assuredly a very fair question which was directed at me; a moment of truth – I had never asked. 'I think he said it was cream in colour,' said I rather lamely, 'though it could be white' (even more lamely). We found it eventually, but were half an hour late, for which we gave profuse apologies. Fortunately the clotted cream had not turned sour.

44

Are We Lucky?

*B*ORN and bred in Devon. I have lived my entire life here except for brief periods, when a young man, working away from the area.

Never have I – or do I – wish to dwell elsewhere. Ann likewise was born in the South West – at Padstow to be exact – though she spent most of her youth in London. However, now she cannot imagine spending her days anywhere other than in this magnificent peninsula.

Still, whilst we agree we will assuredly see out our days amongst the verdant, rolling terrain which surrounds us – and happily so – there is something she often says with which I slightly disagree. For at times when we are out and about, the sun beaming down on the countryside all around, the grandeur of Dartmoor towering above us, she will opine, 'We are so lucky to live here.'

Granted in environmental terms I know of no better place to pass one's days, nowhere in Britain in which the air is purer, the grass greener, the rural roads, generally, less cluttered, the pace of life more relaxed. This, though, surely is only part of the picture; certainly such are vital aspects when pursuing a fulfilling, civilised lifestyle, but only a portion of a much larger whole. It is said that 'man and woman cannot live by bread alone'; correct – but neither can they live solely by absorbing natural beauty and fresh air.

The means to make a decent living, an infrastructure of roads, railways, airports in keeping with this sophisticated, high-tech era, plus access to high quality theatre, art, music and culture in general, are crucial to folk being able, fully, to experience the best our great country can, and does, provide. Sadly so much of this is lacking in the South West peninsula; good, secure, well paid work, likewise. Some districts in Devon and the Duchy endure, on average, the lowest incomes in the land; true there is little unemployment, but so much of the work is poorly paid.

Thus young people leaving school, when seeking careers and salaries which can give them a fulfilling and progressive lifestyle, often move away. Many would love to remain here, but are persuaded to forsake the South West – if not forced to – by the limited opportunities, plus the reality, amongst other considerations, they so often cannot afford a house. The double whammy here is that whilst numerous local people cannot make the increasingly difficult leap onto even the lowest rung of the property ladder, legions from outside the area can – and do. They retire from well paid work in the South East, the Midlands, even the North and come to the beautiful South West to see out their days.

They have both the means and desire to buy homes in Devon and Cornwall, thus push up the price of dwellings at every level. Granted virtually every new building development has to have a percentage (usually low) of 'affordable' housing, but even these are often beyond the pocket of a majority of local young men and women. In a free country, of course, citizens have the right to move wherever they wish, but it cannot be pretended that an influx of those of a senior generation coming to retire, replacing many of the younger element whose energy, ambition and skills are the life blood of communities, is a positive movement. Also it puts strain on health and care facilities in the region.

It would help if a reasonable proportion of those coming West were of working age, thus able to fill gaps in terms of skills and expertise. Sadly, relatively few fall into this category. In the specialised world of professional football, this has long been the case; Plymouth Argyle have always struggled when it comes to enticing players to Home Park; they might forsake the North or Midlands in their later years, but career-wise they treat the prospect of moving to an outpost such as the Ocean City as being akin to going to Outer Mongolia.

Children and youth who inhabit the Peninsula are also on the end of an unjust deal; for the grants per head from government for education are, for some inexplicable reason, lower than anywhere else in Britain.

That this article has been one long moan, I cannot deny, but I feel in numerous ways Devonians and the Cornish are not treated as fairly as we have a right to expect. So whilst I've no desire to live elsewhere, and don't envy those who inhabit other regions, I don't consider myself to be especially lucky.

45

Ringing the Changes

*D*OORBELLS have featured quite prominently in my
life. For many years I was a door-to-door salesman
and insurance agent; thus it was crucial to my living that I
be able to raise the occupants of a dwelling.

Also, for even longer, I was a local councillor; so every
four years I had to attempt to disturb the peace of good,
honest folk for the totally selfish act of trying to persuade
them to cast their vote in my direction (in retrospect, it might
have been a counter-productive intrusion on their time).

Over the decades, I've encountered scores of different
sounds and blasts after pushing the button; there are those
so soft they appear pointless, others with a blast which
could shake doors; and the musical ones. Our national
anthem is popular, as, it would seem, are those of some
foreign lands, which doesn't impress this chauvinistic old
man; patriotic renderings are not rare – 'Land of Hope'
and Glory', 'Jerusalem' and 'Rule Britannia' abound.
Hymn tunes, also, such as 'Onward Christian Soldiers',
the 'Hallelujah Chorus' and one which often gives comfort
to Argyle supporters, 'Abide With Me'.

Further snatches of melody can range from Mozart to Johnny Cash, Beethoven to Roy Orbison, Sousa to the Laurel and Hardy theme. Having stated all this, the main thrust of this article is to pinpoint the negative – not to highlight the numerous sounds bells emit, but rather the great number which make no noise at all. Though I've not made a detailed survey of such, it is my humble opinion that at any given time, up to 25 per cent of these crucial domestic alerts (some appearing quite new and sophisticated) do not work. To be fair, at times the pusher cannot be absolutely certain if they are operating or not, for it could be the alarm is sounding, but can only be heard internally – though a barking dog will often give clues in this direction; at times, one's presence on a doorstep can be signalled by usage of a door knocker – though these vary greatly in both size and effectiveness. Some are of a vastness which might be sufficient to break down doors in the Tower of London, whilst others are so puny they'd not swat a fly.

At home we were fortunate, for our bell, installed long ago, whilst eschewing melodic and eccentric sounds, was exceptionally reliable. Then a while back – calamity; giving in to age, it ceased to work. It was a system which operated directly from mains electricity; thus we asked an electrician to give a price for a replacement; his quote was such we looked for other options. A battery operated system seemed the best – well, the cheapest anyway. It was purchased, installed, and appeared to 'tick all the boxes'; it was quite loud, reasonably melodic, and seemed reliable. The trouble, however, was that its life turned out to be short. For fewer than three months following its

h

affixing, there was an almighty hammering on the front door. Opening it, I found a gent standing upon the step, holding a large parcel. 'Sorry to bang so loudly, but the bell's not working,' said he.

I made no attempt to hide my surprise. 'But it's almost new,' I cried – then gave it a push myself; complete silence.

'Is it a battery one?' he enquired. I nodded. 'Waste of money,' he opined. 'It's always happening – batteries run out in no time. You need to be connected to the mains.'

That this was sound advice we did not doubt – this gent clearly spent half his life trying to alert householders to his presence at their door. However, we did not act on it. For just a few weeks earlier, as a birthday present, I had been given a battery charger (which had not been received with excessive joy as I could neither eat or drink it). This. though, could be salvation. Ann worked out how to operate it, so we set about recharging. It worked. The batteries re-inserted, the bell sang lustily; sadly, though, for but a week. We would not be defeated; fresh ones were bought, and again the bell was powered to trill merrily – for just a fortnight.

The bullet has been bitten; we have invested in a fully electrical system. It's working at present – but it was installed less than a month ago; watch this space.

46

Farmers & Farming

A GENT asked me recently as to why I had never gone farming, even though it had been in my family for so very long; a fair question.

Generations, on both my father's and mother's side, have worked holdings in the Tamar Valley, keeping livestock and growing that wide range of fruit, flower and vegetable crops for which, until relatively recently, this lovely, historic valley was famed.

My brother, Stan, who from early childhood wished nothing other than to make a living from the land, has done so for over 60 years now.

I cannot say I did not have the opportunity, as being the youngest of three sons, I almost certainly would have had the chance of taking over our farm at Bere Alston when my parents retired. There are various reasons why I chose not to but principal amongst them is the fact my desire to work the land was never robust enough to overcome my doubts regarding spending the rest of my days pursuing a way of life which demanded unrelenting dedication to gruelling work, total commitment in terms of time, plus comprehensive knowledge – and, not least, with uncertain financial rewards.

Mind you, if I had been the son of landed gentry rather than working farmers, then, being a man who has always found physical labour daunting, I could well have viewed matters differently. For I am very much a country lad; if I'd been born the local squire able to trundle around a large, rolling Devonshire estate in my Range Rover, having the occasional chat with my estate manager, there is a strong probability I would have welcomed the life; thus the manifold, often ill considered ways I've attempted, over the decades, to 'earn my crust' would not have transpired.

The livings made by my parents and their forebears, however, were to some extent based on the shedding of 'blood, sweat and tears'.

Up until well into the 20th century, a majority of farmers and growers in the valley were tenants of the local landlord. Eventually my grandparents were able to buy their farm; likewise my parents, though they also were tenants for the first years of their marriage. They were highly competent custodians of livestock and astute workers of the land – something I was aware of at an early age. Also I was mindful that such expertise meant little if not accompanied by stoicism and a disciplined resolve. I knew only too well that I did not, and never would, possess such qualities.

The cussedness of the natural world has perpetually irked me; why can't a cow be milked once a week rather than twice every day of the year? Why doesn't a ewe, when giving birth, do so in sunshine at, say, midday, rather than in the early hours of a foul winter's night? Why is it that grass is cut for hay in the noble interests of feeding stock in the dark days yet often is ruined by the malevolence of adverse weather or a field of tall, golden wheat laid low by a thunderstorm? In horticulture again the elements can bring calamity – financial as well as ecological. A field of daffodils in spring – suddenly unseasonably warm weather, causing the blooms to open faster than they can be picked and sent to market; likewise strawberries in June, a heatwave ripening fruit so rapidly, the bulk will remain, ungathered, on the plants. Conversely, here could be a spell of rain which will rot the succulent berries. Also acres of potatoes can be destroyed by blight, or their harvest in early autumn hindered by excessive precipitation, and that most vital of vegetables needs to be gathered before winter as it is vulnerable to frost.

So a most precarious way to make a living; indeed, could any be more so; for in most jobs and professions one can, to a considerable extent, guide one's own fortunes.

Hard work, sound judgement, attention to detail plus common sense will, generally, bring reasonable success. Farming and growing, however, are so different, for no matter how assiduous and skilled one is in pursuing one's craft, the 'slings and arrows of outrageous fortune' weather-wise – all beyond the control of workers of the land – can wreak havoc, even bring bankruptcy.

So why does anybody do it? Not easy to answer. It is, though, a special way of life – one of individuality and rugged independence.

At its best, also, there can be immense pride and fulfilment; a fine herd of cows, a prolific 'crop' of lambs in the spring; a rich field of barley or a heavily laden, succulent plot of strawberries.

Such would bring a great sense of achievement to my parents, one I can almost envy – and one which they richly deserved.

47

A Linguistic Minefield?

*T*HERE was a tale I heard recently concerning a foreign student at a British university trying to master English. This is essential to some extent, as our native tongue is undoubtedly the nearest there is to being universal; the fact it is largely the worldwide computer language is hugely relevant to this.

The poor chap worked long and hard but, in the essay he submitted to his tutor, had made many errors in terms of the use of words. When this was pointed out to him he was both frustrated and bemused – 'but I used the spell check,' said he.

The fact was, though, that he had not spelt words incorrectly, but, rather, had employed the wrong ones – something no computer could detect. One has to sympathise with him and anyone else trying to master our complex written and spoken vocabulary – for so many terms sound the same, yet have very different meanings.

The examples are manifold; the Queen 'reigns' over us, the Lord 'rains' upon us, whilst 'reins' guide a horse. The ''oss' could be called upon to pull a wagon which is 'stationary' but as it cannot write, will have no need of 'stationery'. It is probable that this animal will not, like us, become 'bored' but when being transported will 'board' a horse box.

The Shire breed of the equine, being large, will have a considerable 'waist', and because it will eat a large amount will leave behind plenty of 'waste'. If abused the beast might aim a 'deliberate' kick at its abuser but it's unlikely to have sufficient intelligence to 'deliberate' on any matter requiring deep thought. It could be it would drink water from a 'pail' but as its skin is covered in hair, its face will never appear 'pale'.

Whilst it will probably be housed in a 'stable', if the animal is highly strung there is a possibility its temperament will be far from 'stable'; if it is a racehorse, it will spend time galloping across a 'plain' but it is highly unlikely it will ever board a 'plane'.

If this long suffering creature gets injured it could well suffer 'pain' and might be confined to its stall where it will have to view the world through a window 'pane'.

If unwell it would probably be put on a special 'diet' but it would never join a 'diet', a legislative assembly often connected with the church. When fit, these strong beasts are able to 'bear' great burdens but formidable though they might be they would probably come out second best when confronted by a 'bear'; in this direction they are not helped by the fact they wear no clothes or protection – they are 'bare'.

Horses do not go on stage so they will never take a 'bow' but might wear one attached to their harness to denote success in a show; it'll have nothing much to do with a 'bough', though, unless it falls from a tree onto its head.

'I thought we were going for a ride on the "plain"!'

Mind you, it's not only foreigners who have trouble with the Anglo Saxon language; vast numbers of us, born, bred and schooled in these islands will have words – often many – which perplex.

A mind-concentrating one to me, I solve by reciting to myself (when I can remember it), that 'all school 'principals' should have high 'principles'.'

However, I can never get my head around the difference between 'practise' and 'practice'. According to the dictionary, they do differ but so subtly it is beyond my obtuse intelligence to comprehend how. Likewise 'licence' and 'license' – I used to work with a gent, extremely erudite, who tried to explain the difference. He failed.

There are numerous other words quite similar in terms of spelling and sound which have dramatically different meanings. For example, a body is 'interred' in a grave, but a suspected enemy of the state is 'interned'.

There are folk who are difficult to locate – they are 'elusive" If, however, they are 'illusive', their very existence could be in doubt.

'Draught', too, is another which can cause confusion; for it can be cold air blowing under a door or a pint of real ale drawn from a cask; and a 'draft' can be a rough sketch or an invitation (which cannot be refused) to join the Army.

We have a word here in the South West which almost invariably causes confusion to those not born here – 'directly'. Those not used to our ways – or vernacular – assume it denotes immediate action. To we local folk, though, it generally means the opposite. . . '*manyana*'. Still, we do have the grace to pronounce it differently – 'dreckly'.

48

Follow Your Dreams

*A*MONGST my many failings is an ineptitude when it comes to giving advice. Mind you, it's not that important as rarely has such been sought from me – either from the wider world or, more importantly, from my family.

This to me is a relief as I've never felt equipped to give it, especially when it came to my sons in terms of education and career paths. More pertinently, perhaps, I feel I would have been a hypocrite if I had done so. For I'm a man who has seen (foolishly and wrongly) formal education and training as being an impediment to, and intrusion in one's life rather than the vital ingredient regards success, progress and self esteem which, clearly, it is indeed. I did not so much leave school as escape from it.

Strangely though, many years later I felt the desire to seek a little more learning, so pursued a correspondence course, gaining two A-levels; then a further one in which I managed a degree. Being the somewhat solitary, miserable toad I am, I quite enjoyed studying in the informal isolation of a room in our house, whereas the disciplined uniformity of a well populated classroom definitely lacked allure. Sadly my mature academic attainments did nothing for me career-wise. A-levels in history and English literature, then a degree in history do not contribute much when it comes to following well paid, long term employment; thus have I never had a profession or trade, or formal training of any kind. The upshot is I've perpetually done 'jobs' and as I've ever lacked 'stickability', they have been many and varied.

My wife, Ann, however, is very different; an intelligent lady of vision and perception she was, and remains, most able in all aspects of life, included in which is the giving of sound advice to our family – especially our sons when it is sought. Certainly, many years back, she encouraged them, strongly, to seek degrees and qualifications – three of them attaining the former, the other a high level of qualification as a craftsman. Thus all have achieved, and continue to do so, for which I give thanks, and in two directions – the wisdom of Ann's guidance and for their determination, hard work, ambition and good sense.

Assuredly had they come to me back in their youth seeking my views as to the paths they should take in life, my counselling would have been different; due, most likely, to my jaundiced and biased view of formal education (which I've never been able to shed), it is probable I would have taken a somewhat 'laissez faire' approach – 'follow your dreams', or words to that effect, might well have come from my lips if any son had asked for help regarding their forward path.

If they had wanted to join a circus to become a trapeze artist, or take up brush, oils and canvas to paint landscapes for a living, or even to sail single handedly around the world, then more than likely I'd have said, 'Do it.' Ann, also, might well have stated the same but would have suggested, strongly, the pursuance of such desires be delayed until they had gained the education, knowledge and training to make a decent living.

For a majority of us will, for many years, have responsibilities for others – children, spouses, partners; mortgages to pay, stomachs to be filled, clothes to be bought, plus a multitude of other insistent demands on one's purse in this modern age. Following a dream might well be a romantic and satisfying concept but so often it will fail to swell bank accounts; as a gentleman I knew used to say – somewhat forlornly – 'once I thought that life was beauty but then I found that life is duty.'

Mind you, once educated, there is good sense in young folk delaying the up-taking of commitment; for instance, many leave university or formal training then back-pack around the globe, seeing other cultures, seeking diverse experiences. This, in a sense, is the pursuance of dreams; however, unlike muddle-headed old fools such as myself, theirs will be personal desires which, whilst fulfilling, do not obscure the realities of a tough, demanding world.

It was possibly that famed writer and poet, Rudyard Kipling, who summed it up, succinctly, in his masterly 'If', with the advice to his son (all sons and daughters, for that matter) – 'if you can dream but not make your dreams your master.'

Wise words – yet ones I've always found hard to heed. For instance, I still dream that Plymouth Argyle will one day be successful – though perhaps 'hallucinate' would be a more apt term.

49

The Sticking Plaster

REGULARLY do our newspapers and media carry major items regarding our overburdened health and care services – people having to wait weeks for appointments, longer for treatment, operations and the like.

Even more alarming is that folk can spend hours sitting in hospital accident and emergency departments awaiting attention from a medic. Now, much adverse criticism – rightly to an extent – comes the way of governments and health authorities regarding this grave situation, but my observation is that rarely does anybody question why this situation exists; could it be that, overall, the health of the nation is deteriorating? Granted we are living longer now, which clearly puts extra strain on the medical profession, but surely this is not the sole cause.

A clue to a contributory factor came my way a few weeks ago when a friend told me of a mishap which had recently come his way.

On his way to work, he tripped on a loose flagstone in the pavement; falling heavily he gashed his hand. Arriving at his office, he washed the cut then searched the first aid box for a sticking plaster – to no avail. There were bandages sufficient to swathe a dozen mummies – but no plasters. When he enquired as to why, he was told that such were prohibited in offices, factories and the like, as a person attaching one to their wound might suffer an allergic reaction.

His hand clearly still needing attention, he went to a prominent chemists in the town and bought a packet of plasters. The attachment of this clearly needed the use of both hands; as one of his was the destination for the dressing, he needed assistance; not unreasonably, he sought the help of members of the staff in the shop. None was forthcoming; it was not that the assistants were callous or unhelpful – it was the rules; the monster that can be 'health and safety' had struck again.

The reason given was that not one of the staff present had been on a first aid course, therefore no one was qualified to affix the plaster. Thus, in theory, if he needed assistance it was up to him to find someone suitably trained.

He returned to his place of work bemused and still bleeding; explaining the bizarre situation to his colleagues, he was overwhelmed by a laudable surge of the 'Dunkirk Spirit' plus an admirable pursuit of the creed, 'a friend in need is a friend indeed'. Numerous hands were thrust forth to aid the attachment of the plaster, even though none had been on the sacred first aid course – the indomitable spirit of the British race at its best.

As yet there has been no summons from the authorities to appear before a court of law despite this flagrant breaching of the rules – though it could still happen.

However, this has concentrated the minds of Ann and myself – serial sticking plaster users. As we get older, we seem to cut more easily; rarely does a sojourn in the garden cease without one of us needing a gash or deep scratch covered, especially upon hands. In the past, the victim has always been attended to by the one of us who has escaped injury. What, though, to do in the future? Neither of us has the qualification apparently required by law; we have discussed it and come to a decision; though basically law abiding citizens, we will continue to place relevant dressings upon each other until we are prosecuted (though this is not easy as it ever seems a fraught operation removing a plaster from its packaging).

This perverse experience of my friend, however, brings me back to a possible clue – mentioned in the early part of this article – as to why A and E departments are so crowded. Could it be that some patients attending these emergency units need just a light dressing or a sticking plaster placed upon them but have no family member or friend who has undergone first aid training? Thus, unwilling to contravene regulations, they sit in waiting rooms – sometimes for hours – awaiting such minor attention? Also it is not inconceivable that, if they have no transport of their own, they have summoned an ambulance – possibly even the flying one – to deliver them for treatment?

With such medical statutes and so many other petty safety rules which bedevil our lives, one has to pose the question – 'are the lunatics finally in charge of the asylum?'

50

The Sounds of Christmas

*T*HE sound of the cuckoo, plus sight of swallows herald the coming of spring, whilst the departure of the latter tells us autumn is nigh; the arrival of avocets on the Tamar is the harbinger of winter.

Following this, in early December, we will hear the warbling of the 'Bing' bird. This species has but one specimen – a male – and he, despite the fact he died many years ago, is to be heard singing a melodious ditty in which he expresses a desire for cold weather – especially during the upcoming, much enjoyed and anticipated annual midwinter festival.

The full name of this songster is Bing Crosby (I've no idea what that is in Latin), and he is dreaming of a 'White Christmas'.

Mind you, whilst a snowy Yuletide has a certain romance about it, the reality is this icy substance looks better on a festive card than on a road or pavement; on those it can cause chaos.

Whatever, when Bing's soothing crooning massages the ears, one is aware that Father Christmas and his helpers are getting into top gear. Meanwhile, the reindeer will be on extra hay rations as they move towards peak fitness for their prodigious journey around the globe, which has to be undertaken overnight on Christmas Eve.

Also, to my mind, Bing's desire for the white stuff marks the beginning of what, to me, is one of the finest aspects of this potentially joyous season – the playing of festive music, especially the carols.

My favourite radio station is Classic FM and they generally can be relied upon to delight the senses – well, mine at least – with the playing of the traditional 'Once in Royal David's City', 'Silent Night', 'Oh Come All Ye Faithful' – I never tire of hearing them. Likewise of the insomniac shepherds watching their flocks, the three kings from the Orient (not Leyton, I'm reliably informed), the merry gentlemen whom God is exhorted to rest, the listening out for the 'herald angels', the bleak winter weather with its frosty wind 'making moan', the forays of Good King Wenceslas to alleviate the hardships of the poor – I enjoy all these, while numerous other musical expressions dedicated to the celebration of the birth of Christ appeal immensely.

Having said this, there are a number of seasonal songs, not really religious, which also appeal; 'The Twelve Days of Christmas' is one – though how the 'true love' manages to despatch to the lady in his life such extraordinarily varied gifts as partridges in pear trees, lords a leaping, humming birds, ladies dancing and the like, is a mystery. Our excellent Royal Mail might find it a major challenge; after all, how can anybody guarantee delivery of geese in the act of laying?

'There's 363 more items to come!'

Amongst others, Cliff Richard has recorded some pleasant seasonal melodies, whilst Santa's invitation to Rudolph to utilise his glowing nose to guide the sleigh has a certain charm, as does Harry Belafonte's lovely ballad, 'Mary's Boy Child'.

However, being a moaning old toad, I must say there are several Christmas songs which have little appeal to me. Some pop groups belt out numbers with seemingly banal, repetitive lyrics; often such are meant to convey messages of hope and goodwill, but in my opinion do not gel.

Then there are the trite seasonal songs – often more froth, than beer. We have our share in these islands, but fortunately they do not proliferate as they do in the United States. Two years ago, Ann and I spent Christmas in New York with our son Matthew, daughter-in-law Avisa and their three children. Thanks to their hospitality, we had a magical time, but seasonal music to please our senses was virtually non-existent. A puzzling paradox regarding Americans would seem to be that whilst they are amongst the most overtly Christian nations on earth, they often seem to ignore the fact that December 25 is the day we celebrate the birth of Jesus. Thus one does not hear carols as such, or any vocals that really articulate as to what the celebrations are about; 'happy holiday' is the greeting from the lips of many folk and often is what is emblazoned on seasonal cards, whilst the songs are the likes of 'Frosty the Snowman', or worse.

Still, this year, it will be very much back to normal – three weeks of traditional carols, then, on Christmas Eve, a comfortable chair to sit in, glass in hand and a delightful hour watching the choir from Cambridge, in exquisite harmony, exuding an aura of peace and hope to a somewhat troubled world

51

There's No Place Like Home

*T*HAT much lauded eighteenth century writer and lexicographer, Doctor Samuel Johnson, was a man famed and remembered as much for that which he said as for what he wrote.

Mischievously, and probably provocatively, he stated that 'the finest sight a Scot ever sees is the road which leads to England'. In this era of Scottish nationalism and the like, I'll opt for caution and make no comment. However, possibly Johnson's best known and most quoted observation was to state in his unequivocal, highly opinionated way, that he [or she] who is tired of London is tired of life'.

Although I would suggest that such a view is a touch dramatic and over the top, nonetheless I can see from whence he came when declaiming this.

Undoubtedly there are numerous fine cities around the globe which I have never seen (and assuredly will not visit now), but I have been to the likes of New York, Paris, Beijing, Hong Kong, Budapest and Berlin. Whilst all have considerable and diverse qualities – many of which are unique – and are rewarding destinations for the tourist,

London, to me, is supreme – a metropolis awash with the history and heritage of a great nation.

I first spent some time in the capital during the early 1960s when, for a few months, I worked there. A country boy to whom Smeaton's impressive tower on Plymouth Hoe was the height of venerability, I spent virtually every spare minute I had visiting, absorbing, relishing, feasting on all the almost legendary edifices and landmarks which then, and now, remain central to one's feelings of nationhood, pride and patriotism.

Buckingham Palace and the Changing of the Guard, St Paul's, Westminster Abbey, The Tower of London, Whitehall and the Houses of Parliament, 10 Downing Street (one could almost walk up to its front door in those less security conscious times), the Cenotaph and so much more, the listing of which would fill the rest of this article and beyond.

Even then, though, I saw but a fraction of the sights – this massive metropolis has an abundance and variety which it is possible no other conurbation can match.

During the ensuing half century-plus since then, I've been able to increase my knowledge of London. The principle acquisition of this awareness is due to the fact that Ann spent most of her youth living there and knows the city well. Thus on our visits, using the excellent underground system, she acts as guide. She is assisted in this by our eldest son, Neill, who has lived there now for well over 30 years.

Regularly do we spend long weekends with him, our lovely daughter-in-law, Debbie, and our cherished granddaughter, Jasmine. Their hospitality is such that staying at the Ritz would be a downwards step. It goes beyond this, though, as we accompany them to eminent locations we've never before seen. Also, on occasions, tickets are obtained, almost magically, for renowned sporting venues – Wembley, Lords, The Oval and, assuredly not least as far as Ann is concerned, Wimbledon.

Now, long-suffering, stoic readers of my regular meanderings could well be sitting in Tavistock, Okehampton and beyond East Cornwall, *newspaper* in hand, wondering what relevance to anything has this ramble eulogising our mammoth capital city.

Well, herein lies an odd paradox; for although we both savour our long weekends in Battersea in the cosseted company of our much loved family, it seems, strangely, to strengthen our ties with our South West peninsula.

Perhaps, to a degree, it can be summed up by the old adage that 'parting is such sweet sorrow'; for whilst we miss them, we do not pine for London.

Speaking for myself, being very much a rural lad, I've never had any major desire to live amidst this vast urban sprawl, sophisticated and state-of-the-art though much of it is. Thus, when our visits are over and we make for the M3, we feel a mild form of relief and relaxation. Turning onto the A303, such positive thoughts increase – we are heading west.

Stonehenge is reached and passed, invariably slowly. Why so many folk pay good money to stand in all weathers, staring at a pile of stones has long been beyond me.

Usually the rest of the journey home will see traffic moving at a more leisurely pace – as does life itself, in this part of the world – for so much of the highway is single-lane. Inexorably, though, we are moving towards our glorious county.

Then suddenly, at the end of a dual carriageway hardly longer than a football pitch, a sign to elevate the spirits: Devon. Mind you, usually it will be raining.

52

Cards on the Table

*L*IKE many other folk this Christmas, we festooned our sitting room walls with the cards we received.

It was an inspiring array of fat robins, portly Santas snowy and frosted landscapes, brightly illuminated trees, myriad reindeer, jolly looking Dicken's characters, even some which point towards the true meaning of the occasion, the celebration of the birth of Christ. Hung on twine and pinned to the wooden rail at the top of the walls, there were not, however, quite sufficient to completely go around the room and thus the symmetry was disturbed.

A solution, though, struck me as we took down the cards and decorations on Twelfth Night. Next Yuletide we can augment the Christmas card display by hanging up the numerous invitations we receive to donate to charities, many of which are brightly-hued and reasonably seasonal greetings cards.

Usually it is October when they start to arrive and by the middle of November, the excellent ladies and gents who deliver the mail can be seen staggering down our path bearing bundles of envelopes, so many of which exhort us to give generously to their cause.

Early on there is often communication from the mouth and foot artists with samples of their work, followed by a plethora of requests to support causes ranging from the high-profile to the obscure. The blind, deaf, various medical research projects; hospices – especially children's – disabled groups, those dedicated to helping people with psychiatric problems. The good causes are myriad and numerous.

There are organisations dedicated to the underprivileged and homeless, others providing holidays for orphans and the like. This Christmas, we received a request from the National Trust to assist in the funding of some dilapidated old mansion, which, as Ann and I are members and pay a three figure sum annually for the privilege – was not sympathetically received.

There are, too, manifold groups concerned for the welfare of citizens of the Third World. Rightly or wrongly, I give my financial support to none, as I adhere to the adage that 'charity begins at home'. Not that I am uncaring; it is just that we as a nation give more in official foreign aid than virtually any other country – something we should be proud of; so. as such comes from the taxes we pay, each of us indirectly contributes towards helping the deprived in distant lands

In consequence, any charitable donations I make, which I do – although Ann makes more – have to be to those societies that strive to improve the lives of Britons of all ages. Whilst the numbers of such are high, those dedicated to the wellbeing of animals would appear to be greater. . . cats and dogs homes, donkey sanctuaries, the likes of the

j

PDSA which ministers to sick creatures, plus a multitude of others whose aim is to bring succour to beasts and birds, great and small. Also there are groups dedicated to the protection of endangered species in foreign lands, especially Africa. Though sympathetic to these causes, I feel these are issues which must be tackled by the Governments and peoples of these lands.

Now there are some requests which I find a touch bizarre. To the fore of these was one which came in December seeking support for a group I had never before encountered: World Horse Welfare – based in Britain although it appeared to concern itself with equines around the globe. Prominent amongst the literature sent, was a sketch of a healthy looking 'oss with a woolly scarf around its neck. Why the muffler, I know not. It wasn't explained. Is the purpose of the charity to raise money to provide scarves for all horses? Who knows? I assuredly made no effort to find out.

Whilst I cannot comment on the rest of the world there are already numerous folk in these islands who dedicate themselves to the well-being of these fine animals – and who would, probably, provide them scarves if necessary!

If this all sounds like a rather jaundiced view of charitable organisations, the great majority of which do good in the world, it is not intended. It is, though, perhaps a plea for folk to be left in peace next Christmas, for them to give (or, indeed, not to give) in accordance with their means and desires – it is not a time to be harassed. Mind you, I do have a suggestion for a new charity – one devoted to the comfort of miserable, moaning, grumpy old men. If a card from them arrives next Christmas, it will join the others on the string around the wall. . . in pride of place!

53

Price of Progress

MANY years ago there was an absorbing Hollywood film entitled 'Inherit the Wind'; it starred that fine actor Spencer Tracy, playing a lawyer. Its theme concerned religious fundamentalism and how mindsets have to move on if progress is to be made. Tracy's character points out there is usually a price to pay for the forward movement of humanity; amongst many other examples he employs man's mastery of aviation using the perceptive and evocative sentence: 'Yes, you can learn to fly, but the birds will lose their wonder and the clouds will smell of gasoline.'

Nowadays, being an old man in a world in which galloping technological advances cause rapid, radical changes in habits and behaviour, those insightful words frequently come to my mind.

To say I have no regrets over our changing way of life would not be true, but I have ever been a pragmatist, never burdened with the frustrations of being idealistic.

So my musings lead me to the conclusion that so much of the revolution in the way folk go about their daily routines probably makes their lives easier, saving time and energy which can be devoted, in theory, to that which will fulfil, avoiding many wearisome tasks which can clutter a day. After all, why trudge to the bank when you can conduct your financial affairs online? Why go to the post office and dispatch a letter when you can send emails, texts and the like which will reach someone instantly, even if they're on the far side of the globe? Why brave foul winter weather – indeed, waste time any month of the year – in travelling to and meandering around supermarkets when again the use of cutting edge technology means customers can order from the comfort of their armchairs, then receive the delivery at their front doors?

Granted, dinosauric technophobes such as myself still have to do things the laborious, historic way, but clearly we are becoming an endangered species. Clothes, books, furniture – indeed, virtually anything and everything – can now be ordered over the ether and brought to one's doorstep. Not surprisingly vast numbers make use of such; paradoxically, however, many of these will bemoan the demise of shops on the high street, the closure of bank and building society branches and, of course, post offices, especially in rural locations.

A lady I know is outraged at the reduction in library services, yet she herself never visits them, doing most of her reading from a Kindle. Assuredly the old adage, 'use it or lose it', covers, vividly, this scenario.

There can be little doubt we are experiencing, in effect, a revolution and, as in all such upheavals, there are casualties and victims – most of them innocent. In the retail sector, thousands are losing their jobs, whilst many small shopkeepers are going out of business.

So many streets are disfigured with empty shops, offices and the like – certainly a situation of negativity and dismay.

Yet there can be a positive side; despite such job losses there is little unemployment, because if one does lose their job then other opportunities occur. For example, goods ordered on line have to be packed in a warehouse or super-market, then delivered; folk will be employed to fulfil these services.

A majority of us enjoy increased leisure time, go on more holidays, eat out more often; thus additional staff are needed to meet such demands.

Former retail outlets in shopping areas are being converted into restaurants and hotels, whilst even in this online age, there will ever be openings for emporiums stocking the unusual, the exotic plus that at the top of the market and, conversely, goods at bargain prices.

Specialist food stores also continue to attract. Mind you, having said all this, there is a direction in which society appears to be moving which, personally, causes concern.

It is the rise in vegetarianism and veganism. In a free society, folk naturally have the right to pursue the diet they desire. The reality, though, is that if a large percentage of the population become vegans, then the countryside as we know it will, to an extent, inevitably cease to exist.

Livestock such as sheep and cattle could be as rare as hedgehogs; after all, no farmer is going to keep a ewe if there is no market for its wool, or the flesh of its progeny, or a cow if no demand for milk, beef and leather. If they did so, bankruptcy invariably would follow. 'Food' for thought?

54

On Your Buzzers

MUCH of television tends to be dominated by quite a
narrow range of subjects. Prominent amongst them
are baking and cooking. There are a plethora of programmes
with chefs showing us how to cook plus competitions in the
fields of haute cuisine and the making of cakes.

Probably the reason why so many media hours are
devoted to the subject is simply that these shows attract
large numbers of viewers.

The irony, though, is that we as a nation cook less than
most, preferring to eat out or fetch takeaways; indeed, in
numerous kitchens the cooker is used about as often as the
fire extinguisher – though the ping of a microwave might
well be heard with monotonous regularity.

House programmes, too, proliferate – those showing
how homes can be improved, others showing desirable
locations to which folk might wish to move. Prominent
amongst the latter is 'Escape to the Country'; the mystery
here is that if so many wish to quit London (which usually
is the case), then why do they pay so much to go to live
there in the first place.

Neither of these subjects hold much interest for myself (especially the latter), whilst my wife Ann, though she views them on occasions, is not an avid follower. What we do watch on a regular basis, however, are quiz shows – Ann possibly more than me. Assuredly there are an abundance to view. As with everything, some appeal more than others; in this, a touch illogically, I feel the presenter is almost as important as the format and the type of questions asked.

'University Challenge' is always a 'must'; wisely the basic rules and composition of the contest have not altered during the 50 years or so it has been running, though there are many differences between the two men who, predominantly, have presided over the decades. The quite genial, enthusiastic Bamber Gascogne was in command for a long time but his place was taken some time ago by a radically different broadcaster, the acerbic Jeremy Paxman. There are those, understandably, who dislike his brusque, often dismissive treatment of contestants but he is adept at ensuring these intelligent students follow the strict rules, plus, vitally I feel, he wastes no time on small talk; also, never does he attempt to be amusing. There is, however, a downside to the show – scarcely do I ever answer a question correctly!

Even more erudite – indeed, arcane – is 'Only Connect', where, I sometimes feel, only members of Mensa have any chance, the questions being so obscure. Ann gets some right but me, never. The programme is in the capable hands of Victoria Coren Mitchell; she is highly intelligent and articulate but has the annoying habit of trying to be funny; in my jaundiced view, she rarely is.

'Mastermind', under the control of the urbane John Humphreys, is a favourite of ours; a criticism, though, is that some of the specialist subjects are so remote and boring, the two minutes of questions seem to last two hours. We both like 'Pointless' the stewardship of which lies in the hands of that amiable and able team, Alexander Armstrong and Richard Osman. Here, more than in most of these knowledge-based shows, there often seems a greater diversity in learning; for some contestants appear to know just about everything whilst others might well struggle to name the Queen.

A quiz which Ann likes but has little appeal for me is 'Eggheads'; not that I fault the actual format; rather I find the question master, Jeremy Vine somewhat annoying – possibly unfairly. It is that, to me, he exhorts too fervently the contestants to beat the experts; indeed, he appears to want them to triumph every time. If they did, logic suggests the programme would soon be shelved; after all, there would be little point in watching learned 'eggheads' who are so very often being beaten.

A show which we both enjoy is 'The Chase'; it has an original style to it and is guided by the excellent Bradley Walsh; efficient, genial, a man of genuine, instant wit, he, I feel, elevates the quiz immensely. There are, of course, a multitude of other such productions ranging from the entertaining to the contrived, plus, to me, the incomprehensible. Also there are versions of these popular shows which, I feel, can devalue them; those where men and women, so often of whom one has never heard, contest under the banner of being 'celebrities'. Often these folk, though probably competent in what they do, appear to have a dearth of general knowledge. Such is modern life but surely it is better – and more entertaining – to watch the basic programmes where, generally, folk are attempting to win a few 'bob' to enhance their lives – perhaps even to pursue their dreams.

55

The Retail Shop

MANY years ago Ann and I took over the leasehold of a small shop close to the centre of Tavistock – she was not keen on doing so, but all too aware of my almost incessant and frankly feckless wanderlust in terms of earning a living, agreed to give it a go.

It turned out, though, she was right to be dubious as to the wisdom of going into retail, for whilst the enterprise did not put us on the path to ruin it produced little profit despite hard work, much effort and long hours on our part.

After some four years we sold on the lease. I had learned a lesson, but in retrospect cannot say I necessarily regret the venture into shopkeeping, even though it had put not 'gold' into our coffers, for it could be said of the clientele of our emporium that to quote the slogan of the now defunct *News of the World* weekly paper 'All Human Life is Here' (well a large percentage of it at least).

Being a man ever interested in the quirks and eccentricities of folk, rich pickings, in terms of memories, came my way via the motley collection of citizenry who came into our store.

Ours was an outlet which stocked a wide range of goods including stationery, greetings cards, local souvenirs, a few toys, general bric-a-brac and a selection of prints, many by the Old Masters. Rarely did a day pass without someone coming in asking questions, making observations and putting forward requests which ranged from the obscure to the obvious, the bizarre to the plain daft. There was a local farmer who I knew, that came in wanting to buy a print hanging in the window – John Constable's 'The Hay Wain' priced at £5. He wanted it as a present for his wife. I handed it to him so that he could see it more clearly, 'Yes, she'll like that,' said he, then he leant forward and enquired 'Be it original?'

I pointed out that had it been we'd not be at that moment running a small shop in Devon but rather sunning ourselves on the terrace of one of our holiday villas dotted around the world.

The sale of greetings cards also regularly brought about almost farcical moments. There was a lady who came in to purchase Christmas cards, stating she wished to have only those which did not in any way refer to Jesus; my pointing out to her that the basic objective of the Yuletide was to celebrate his birth made no impact. She remained insistent that religion should not be involved; I was relieved to be able to sell her a pack of blank cards all sporting pictures of Tavistock.

Another customer was a lady (and the vast majority of the buyers of celebratory stationery were female) who came in one morning and chose a get well card. Just after lunch she was back and swapped the positive missive for one concerning bereavement, the gent who was to be the recipient had expired an hour or so earlier.

A true masterpiece – the shop attracted 'all human life'.

A couple of times messages of goodwill were requested regarding the termination of marriage; one was to wish somebody a 'Happy Divorce' the other 'Congratulations on your divorce'. We were unable to supply such; even I am not as jaundiced as that, and assuredly Ann is not cynical at all.

Possibly the most outlandish request of all on the card front was from someone who wished to purchase an 'In Memorium' to be sent to a friend who had mourned the death of her budgerigar 12 months earlier.

Not being well stocked on such a front, fortunately she was happy with a blank flower strewn effort in which she could pen her own message.

We also stocked more unusual items – some good sellers, others the opposite.

Amongst the former were smallish wall clocks, all of different designs, some almost grotesque; the one thing they had in common was that none ever appeared to keep the correct time.

On the other hand, reluctant to leave our shelves were half a dozen prints of a somewhat eccentric though to me humorous nature. Having not sold any, I gave one to a worthy local charity as a gift for their Christmas raffle. I suffered retribution at the hands of fate for my penny pinching; for having bought a ticket, I won it back.

With its companions it went back on display; it never sold nor sadly did a good deal more which we stocked. Chastened, we have never tried retail again, although it provided us with numerous threads to be woven into the rich tapestry that is life.

56

The Olympic Breakfast

A WHILE back we had three grandchildren staying with us on holiday from New York where they are living at present. The first morning Ann asked them what they would like for breakfast. She anticipated answers along the lines of their choice of cereal, perhaps yogurts, toast, juice and so forth. The reply from one of our granddaughters, the possessor of a magnificent appetite – though this does not lead to overweight as she participates in a wide range of sports (some of them American, I'm saddened to admit) – was not anticipated but very much to the point; 'full English, please.' She was to be disappointed – it was not on the menu.

For in the minds of both Ann and myself, a good fry-up (which I enjoy) is to be had when one is on holiday staying in hotels or B and Bs and is included in the price one pays for the accommodation. Assuredly I indulge myself then, devouring sufficient to ensure that I will need little lunch. Years ago numerous folk would have fried breakfasts before they went to work; in those days, though, vastly more men and women did manual, physically demanding labour – thus needed the 'fuel' of a large meal at the start of day to sustain them. These are very different times, however, with far fewer needing such food early in the morning. Having said this, though, it's clear that whilst their bodies might not require it, and they do not prepare and eat the like in their homes, many folk go to cafes, pubs and restaurants to enjoy the like.

Mind you, the timing of the consuming of these meals is entirely up to the whim of the customer, so many eateries offering 'all day breakfasts'. Their girth is sometimes a clue as to the regularity of their pursuance of such, though not always, of course. Generally the cost of these flavoursome meals is modest – exceptionally so at times. Usually there will be a comprehensive range of these 'full Englishes' in terms of both price and amounts. Although not a buyer of this traditional British fare, often I go into these establishments for a tea or coffee and, out of interest, peruse the menu. Very few threaten sparse rations, whilst the majority give excellent value for money.

Most offer varying sizes of breakfasts; also, gluten free, vegetarian and even vegan versions (though how the last one is created has surely to be masterly in terms of the culinary art).

The difference in amounts, thus calorie content, in the volume of these meals was brought home to me recently when enjoying a beverage in a deservedly popular cafe in the Tamar Valley. Here the options on the 'full English' started with the description, 'small'; with this there seemed to be sufficient to sustain me for a couple of days, whilst the 'medium' one would keep both Ann and I going for a like period. The third option was 'large', which would feed us both for the best part of a week. The final one was described as 'Olympic', well named as it appeared to contain sufficient victuals to feed a dozen Sumo wrestlers. I heard a gent of a quite slender build order one.

The service in this cafe always being swift, within a few minutes his meal was delivered. A young, strongly built waiter staggered past bearing a laden platter the size of which would not have looked out of place on a fork lift truck. The customer put down his newspaper, applied condiments and sauces, then commenced eating – at, I imagine, great length.

Gazing at the menu, I saw itemised the range of foodstuffs he had received for a modest cost. So admiring was I at the appetite of this fellow, I considered congratulating him; however, feeling such a gesture could be misunderstood, I satisfied myself with the recording of that which filled his gargantuan dish; it took some time to write it down. This awesome feast was made up of a gammon steak, two sausages, two eggs, three hash browns, black pudding, fried bread, mushrooms, beans and tomatoes.

Having to be on my way, I paid for my drink then took note of the progress being made by the gourmet; he was doing well, appearing to be up to the challenge of clearing his plate. I noticed, however, that many diners with smaller portions, were not – so much good food was left on their dishes.

Now, the size of meal anyone orders is clearly up to them, but once the platter is put before them, all of it should be eaten. In a world where so many are starving, wasting food, in my view, is nothing less than a sin.

57

Me & My Clobber

ONLY once in my life have I attempted to 'tread the boards'; it was not successful.

Back in my youth, a pupil at Tavistock Grammar School, I displayed an uncharacteristic enthusiasm for something other than skiving and a quiet life; I put my name forward for a place in the upcoming annual school play. Amazingly I was given a part – and quite a prominent one at that.

The name of the drama I cannot recall but I think it came from the pen of a French writer. What I do remember, however, is that I was a complete disaster; a Gielgud or Branagh assuredly I was not; thus, rapidly, I was demoted by the play's producer – our English teacher – from a leading role, to the substitutes' bench.

Eventually, I ended up as the town crier, having but 20 or so words to speak during the entire play – and I only gained this part because the lad who was chosen for it was rushed to hospital the day before the production, falling to appendicitis.

Never since have I had the slightest wish to go on stage,

although I do have admiration for those who do – a tough, uncertain way to earn a crust. However, had I shown some talent and gone on to be a professional actor, if still pursuing my 'trade' today my roles would be most limited – and this is because I would only be able to tackle parts where no change of attire was required; any such alteration in costume would render me incapable of acting it.

It was not always thus, mind you, but in recent years both dressing and the reverse have become ever more taxing – problematical, in fact. There are several reasons for this, not least the fact that almost incessantly I feel the cold; thus do I wear more layers of clothes than anybody else I know. Indeed, when fulfilling doctor's or hospital appointments, I always make a point of arriving early as it takes an age for me to strip down for examination; getting dressed again is an even more laborious task.

The fact that the accumulation of garments which entomb my puny body are virtually knee deep when shed, is but part of the problem.

The natural stiffness which accompanies old age looms large, but this is exacerbated as, falling heavily upon it some years ago, my left shoulder is now largely seized up, greatly restricting movement.

Whatever, the reality is that when arising in the morning, I have to allow myself almost as long a period for dressing as I do for ablutions and breakfast. Also I try to plan my day in terms of garments with the goal of attempting to avoid having to change them – not always easy, clearly.

It would help greatly if there was designed a single garb which one could slip into; it would need to be exceedingly

k

thick, mind you, and have a stout zip. Winston Churchill was often seen wearing something like this back in the war, known at the time as a siren suit. There is something similar today, a creation known, I am told, as a 'onesie'; one of our granddaughters had one and adored it. It would though have been far too flimsy for a cold old toad like me; mind you, it all ended in calamity as one day the zip jammed and refused to lessen its grip. Dramatically – but unavoidably – she had to be cut out of it; it has not been replaced.

So there would appear to be no way in which I can avoid shrouding myself in a bulk of 'clobber' sufficient to sustain life for most on the Polar ice cap in winter.

Mind you, these glaciers are now melting; not good news, of course. Climate change is very much the supreme challenge regarding the future of the human race, and has to be confronted. Personally, though, I face a conundrum; for if the world is warming in such a way, why is it I feel ever colder; even regular injections of whisky – though enjoyable – do nothing towards raising my body temperature.

What might, though, is to be swathed in a duvet like shroud of immense thickness – which brings me back to my early life ineptitude regarding stagecraft. For I've heard of a play in which, for its entire duration, there is a body lying on stage beneath a sturdy blanket. The body neither moves nor speaks; what a marvellous role. No lines to learn, no changing of costume, constant warmth under a swathe of wool, a mention in the list of players plus a few 'bob' as well. If the production ever comes west, I'll audition for the role.

'Isn't he supposed to be soundless?'

58

Self Isolation

SHE tried hard not to show it but a momentary expression of despair, perhaps even horror, flitted across my wife Ann's face. For a news item concerned with the curse that is coronavirus – a subject which, naturally dominates the airwaves – reporting the rapidly unfolding and escalating drama, plus misery and calamity, caught her attention especially, as it did mine. For it was suggested that the Government might, sooner rather than later, request – or worse, bring in legislation to insist – that we citizens of the realm above three score years and ten, 'self isolate', possibly for up to four months.

Clearly the realisation struck her like a meteorite that she would not be able to self isolate on her own – she would have to share such a fate with me; indomitable lady though she is, a chill, almost assuredly, would have hurtled down her spine.

She said nothing, of course – she is far too thoughtful and loyal ever to do so; but to be 'confined to barracks' for weeks on end with a grumpy, moaning old toad who, possibly, would find fault with the Garden of Eden could, quite likely, be deemed by a court as contravening her human rights – perhaps even as mental torture.

Now there is one area of the present crisis where I feel we, in our home, can plead 'not guilty'; that is 'stockpiling'; Ann, being a first class cook, we usually have a freezer well stocked with tasty meals plus the ingredients to create more, whilst our pasta and baked bean reserves are sufficient, though not abundant; the toilet roll situation, also, is under control – just. Mind you, I do have concerns regarding my liquor cupboard; whisky supplies are just adequate at present, but will soon need replenishing. There should, however, be no need for panic in that direction, for whilst Nicola Sturgeon spends, seemingly, half her life firing verbal torpedoes at the British Government, no way is she going to cut off supplies of one of Scotland's premier exports.

One certainty is that one of our splendid sons, or older grandchildren, will get it if necessary. Always have we valued our treasured family but possibly never more than now. From near and far we are receiving phone calls on, almost, a daily basis; those nearby drop in regularly to ensure we have sufficient victuals and are not being laid low by this pernicious malady which has the entire globe in its malevolent grip.

The one offspring who is unable to visit is Matthew, who lives and works in New York; for he, our daughter-in-law, Avisa and three grandchildren are, in effect, 'prisoners' there – domestic travel greatly restricted and all foreign flights cancelled. We think of them and pray all is – and will remain – well.

Where this pandemic will lead us and when it will

end, clearly is unknown; but end it will, and hopefully much sooner than some gloomy (though, possibly, well informed) prophets predict. When it does, we, the nation which survived – indeed, won – two horrific world wars, will fight back and eventually get back to normal. The 'Dunkirk Spirit' will triumph. One small whine I have to make, however, plus question I must ask – granted, trivial amidst the mayhem which prevails – is why at a time when, at last, Argyle are looking to be a fair bet for promotion, did fate decree that all league football be abandoned, probably for months to come. At such times I really do have to ask; 'is there a God in Heaven?'

59

When We Move On

*T*HROUGHOUT my life I've endeavoured to avoid repeating my own mistakes and those which would seem to have been made by others. In neither category have I been particularly successful as on many occasions I've made the same errors I had previously witnessed in people and, even more crass, repeated personal blunders and indiscretions. In one field, though, generally I've got it reasonably right – knowing when to move on.

Amongst the greatest hits of country and western star Kenny Rogers was 'The Gambler' which contains the mind concentrating words, 'know when to walk away, know when to run'; the reality here is that if you can judge, reasonably well, the first, you can avoid the stress involved in the second. Knowing when to change tack, when it's time to close a chapter in one's life, is not easy. For instance, someone has done a job or held an office for a long period – been successful, and fulfilled, in the role; the decision to give it up might be as difficult as any they are ever likely to make – yet often it is the correct one.

So many of the turnings I've taken in life have been

foolish, yet a few years ago I did get it right. This was aided partially by Kenny Rogers' wise words, but even more so by a chat we had with a tour guide some years back when Ann and I enjoyed a magical holiday in South Africa. The gent who looked after us was a fine teller of stories about his country and its leaders over the decades. One of his accounts concerned the greatest South African statesman of the first half of the 20th century, Jan Christian Smuts. This was a fellow as eminent in his land as Sir Winston Churchill was in ours. He had been an MP in the South African parliament – for the same constituency – from the 1890s until the 1950s; thus, most successfully, he had negotiated numerous elections. A further one was called in 1951.

Smuts' agent, sensing change, advised the great man to retire; his words were not heeded. The octogenarian stood – and lost his seat. Distraught, he asked his agent what went wrong, 'Why did the voters forsake me?' The reply? 'They did not; the sad fact is that so many of your loyal supporters are now dead.' The world had moved on, the older generation had become fewer, a younger one with different ideas and priorities had taken their place. No matter how great a figure he had been – the fact he'd been prime minister, in total, for over a quarter century meant nothing. His time had passed – many of his supporters likewise.

Some four plus years ago, in a vastly smaller constituency and arena – Tavistock and West Devon – it occurred to me, being a man in my seventies, I was in danger of outliving a goodly number of those loyal, forgiving folk who had long supported me.

After a chat with Ann, who agreed, I decided to 'ride into the sunset' – to jump before being pushed. It was clearly correct, as some fine councillors, far more able and assiduous than myself, were unseated unexpectedly and sadly. Yet there could not – indeed, should not – be any appeal against it; in a democratic society, the electorate is always right. It would, however, have caused those dedicated public servants grief; I was grateful to be spared such pain.

Right throughout history, though, it has been a fact the 'political graveyard', at every level, has been filled by folk who thought, or were told, they could not be beaten. Such a situation occurs well beyond Westminster and councils, mind you, it happens in virtually every walk of life.

Business people who have prospered thanks to astute, at times visionary, decision making often succumb to the complacency which can come with advancing years; at times a failure to realise the methods which have served them well over the years could have become outmoded.

In the theatre world, household names to whom the limelight is almost like lifeblood, walk on stage in their dotage only to discover they cannot remember their lines, whilst famed opera singers who enjoy the spotlight can often disappoint devoted followers when they can no longer hit the top notes; and there are feted sportsmen and women whose legs can no longer keep pace with their skills.

It is amongst the most difficult actions which anyone can undertake but Kenny Rogers' perceptive lyrics say it all; certainly if you know 'when to walk away' you'll not need 'to run'.

60

Famous Last Words

WILLIAM Shakespeare wrote 'the evil which men do lives after them, the good is oft interred with their bones'. There is much truth in this but also it could be argued that people's final words before death – if recorded – will also be better remembered than the accomplishments in life of he or she who uttered them. Mind you, there is often poetic licence involved in the reportage of those statements, both short and long, with some easier to believe than others.

The Bard of Avon so often had his historical characters, many of whom expired before the end of his plays, making extraordinarily long speeches as they lay dying. Hamlet, for instance, spoke a multitude of words; one feels that if only he had saved his breath, he might well have survived. Julius Caesar was somewhat briefer, though he must have been a resilient fellow to have suffered numerous stab wounds from his enemies, yet still had sufficient consciousness to remonstrate with, originally, his closest ally, 'Et tu, Brute; then die Caesar'; why firstly he spoke in Latin, then in English, has always puzzled.

However, it is possible the playwright was tolerably accurate in his recounting of Richard the Third's final plea at the Battle of Bosworth; unseated from his mount, thus at the mercy of Henry Tudor's forces, he cried out, 'a horse, a horse, my kingdom for a horse.' Before he could find another ''oss' however, he lost his life – and his kingdom.

A fictional character, Sidney Carton, the complex 'hero' of Dickens' 'A Tale of Two Cities', was given a remarkable final sentence to proclaim as he was about to face the guillotine: 'It is a far, far better thing that I do than I have ever done, it is a far, far better rest that I go to than I have ever known.' Cynical old toad that I am, I have ever felt that the chances of anybody actually saying such when faced with a violent demise, would be on the same level as Argyle gaining entry into the Champions League.

A famed heroic Englishman, who did exist, was Horatio Nelson, whose final phrase is amongst the most quoted. Laying mortally wounded, he said to his staunch ally: 'Kismet Hardy' – fate indeed.

Then there is the climatic observation of Charles the First when facing his execution. Due to time spent in West Devon, it is said he prophesied two imminent happenings: 'Tomorrow I shall lose my head – and it will be raining in Tavistock.' The ultimate utterance from William Pitt the Younger, who had become Prime Minister at the age of 24, was said to have been a request for his favourite pie from a local bakery; perhaps he actually ate it and that was what saw him off!

On his death bed, King George V was told by his physician that his health was improving and that soon he would be able to take a holiday in Bognor, to which, it is said, he retorted, 'b- - - - r, Bognor' and promptly expired. If this be true, it was not the finest hour for his personal doctor.

Amongst the most quoted final sentences is one which is assuredly well to the fore of the noblest and most poignant ever spoken: 'I am going outside and may be some time.' So spake Captain Oates, a member of the ill fated team led by Devonport born Captain Robert Falcon Scott, trying to be the first ever to reach the South Pole.

Oates, aware that their supplies were dangerously low, and also that his personal fitness was such he might be a hindrance to their survival, sacrificed himself, as he knew that leaving their tent would mean certain death. Scott himself made a final entry in his diary which spoke volumes as to their hopeless position: 'God, this is an awful place.'

There are; of course, numerous other recorded famed final words, ranging from the profound to the amusing. Possibly my favourite are those spoken by the cantankerous and famously atheistic American film actor and comedian of the pre-war era, WC Fields. It is claimed that lying on his death bed, a friend found him reading the Holy Bible; astonished, the visitor enquired as to why; the magnificent answer? 'Just looking for a loophole!'

As to myself, clearly I have no clue as to what my final comments will be; however, if uttered on a Saturday afternoon and the Pilgrims have just lost, then it could be similar to those of George V – minus Bognor, of course!

A favourite last word from WC Fields.